SUPERIOR TEAMS

Superior Teams

What they are and how to develop them

Dennis C Kinlaw

Gower

Published by
Gower Publishing Limited
Gower House
Croft Road
Aldershot
Hampshire GU11 3HR
England

Gower
Old Post Road
Brookfield
Vermont 05036
USA

Dennis C Kinlaw has asserted his right under the Copyright, Designs and Patents Act 1988 to be identified as the author of this work.

British Library Cataloguing in Publication Data

Kinlaw, D. C. (Dennis C.)
    Superior teams
    1. Teams in the workplace
    I. Title
    658.4'02

ISBN 0 566 07959 3

Library of Congress Cataloging-in-Publication Data

Kinlaw, Dennis C.
    Superior teams : what they are and how to develop them / Dennis
C. Kinlaw.
        p.   cm.
    Includes bibliographical references and index.
    ISBN 0-566-07959-3 (hardcover)
    1. Teams in the workplace.   2. Teams in the workplace–Training
of.   I. Title.
HD66.K562   1998
658.4'02–DC21   97-45183
                                                                                    CIP

Typeset in Palatino by Raven Typesetters, Chester and printed in Great Britain by M.P.G. Books, Bodmin.

Contents

List of figures

Preface

Between 1985 and 1991, I conducted an extensive study to determine the characteristics of superior teams. I published the results in the book, *Developing Superior Work Teams: Building Quality and the Competitive Edge* (Kinlaw, 1991).

I made two assumptions when I conducted the study and published the book. My assumptions were that:

- all organizations were faced with the same primary challenge, how to produce consistently superior services and products
- superior teamwork and superior work teams had been demonstrated to be the only consistent strategies for producing superior services and products.

Now, some five years later, as I am preparing the manuscript of this book, enormous changes have taken place in the global competitive environment, downsizing has entered our everyday vocabulary, and the technology of communication moves us daily towards more and more opportunities for access and links to information. Internet and the Worldwide Web, groupware, video phones, video conferencing, synchronous computer conferencing, and ever so much more, are radically changing the way we think about human interaction and collaboration. Many teams of the future may never meet face to face, but will plan, design, solve problems and make decisions through electronic networks.

During this same period, we have learned more and more about how to develop superior teams and we have learned more and more about how to produce consistently superior services and products. Doing more and better with less and less has become the standard against which all organizations now operate, and working more and more as teams has become their typical organizing principle.

As I was completing my study of superior teams in 1991, total quality management and continuous improvement were in full swing. Central to these initiatives were teamwork and team development. Now, some five years after completing the study, there have arisen a number of new organizational development and management innovations, such as re-engineering, principled leadership, organizational visioning, organizational learning and total communication.

In spite of all the changes that have taken place in the last five years and in spite of all the improvement innovations which have been introduced, I still stand by those two assumptions that I made originally. The demand to improve is even greater today than it was five years ago, and the strategies of teamwork and team development are more clearly the keys to continuous improvement today than they have ever been. What is different now is that we continue to find more opportunities to use teams, different ways to organize teams, better and better performance tools for teams to use, and greater clarity about how to lead and support a team-based organization.

Questions today about teams have little to do with the value of teams and whether teams are the best strategy for making the most of human potential and improving total organizational performance. Few organizational leaders or human resource development professionals doubt the value of teams. The questions they raise today are concerned with how to structure teams, develop teams, prepare teams for superior performance and integrate teams fully into a team-based organization. I have written this new book to respond to these current questions and for the following general reasons:

1   The topics of superior teams and superior team performance are as current today as they ever have been. In spite of the extensive production during the last five years of publications on teams, the power of teams and the development of teams, there is still a void of clear, empirically based models of superior teams that managers and human resource practitioners can use to guide their efforts to form teams, develop teams and improve team performance. This book fills that void.

2   Over the past five years, my colleagues and I have accumulated a large amount of survey data about superior teams and teams that want to be superior. In 1990, I completed the development of the Superior Team Development Inventory. We have used the inventory with hundreds of teams and have proven its utility for helping teams manage their own performance and improvement. In this book, I include the Superior Team Development Inventory and describe how it can be used as a tool for developing superior teams.

3   Over the past five years, my colleagues and I have run several hundred Superior Team Development Workshops™. From that experience we have accumulated a large amount of information about the knowledge, skills, and tools that teams need to become superior teams. I have included information from these workshops in this book.

4   In 1985, when I began my study of superior teams, team formation and development were still new initiatives for many organizations. The interest of human resource development practitioners and organizational leaders at that time was focused largely on getting teams formed and up and running. For many organizations today, the need has moved beyond the initial stages of team formation and development to that of helping teams achieve better and better performance outcomes. A final reason for writing this book is to suggest that

the two concepts, mature teams and superior teams, are related and that superior teams are always mature teams.

Simply put, the reason for this book is that teamwork and team development are still the proven, preferred strategies for making the most of any organization's human resources. These are the strategies which are not limited by the knowledge or skill level of individuals. There is no ceiling to the potential of a team. Through shared information, mutual stimulation, interaction and confrontation, teams can break through any previous limit in learning, creativity and performance.

This book provides for managers and other key people (like trainers and consultants) the practical tools that they require for building superior teamwork and developing superior work teams. The specific assistance that the reader can expect to find in this book consists of the following:

- a clear picture of what teamwork and work teams are
- guidelines for identifying the many opportunities that exist for forming and using teams
- a description of the organizational and leadership strategies required to support teams and a team-centred organization
- a step-by-step sequence for developing superior work teams
- the Model for Superior Team Development and Performance and how to use it in developing superior teams
- a description of the Superior Team Development Inventory and how this inventory can be used to assess and improve team development and performance.

Everything in this book has been derived from the workplace and tested in the workplace. Many of the concepts set forth here are supported and corroborated by other authors, but I did not begin my investigation of teams and teamwork in the library. I began seriously thinking about teams and teamwork when I found myself trying to help organizations build teams and foster teamwork in the face of enormous obstacles and in extraordinarily complex environments. The reader can approach the material in this book confident that it is grounded in the real world of work and certain that the ideas, models, tools and techniques found here can make a demonstrable difference in the total performance of work teams.

This book reflects my conviction that the number one priority of organizations should be to change every work unit into a superior team and to make superior teamwork the norm for organizational behaviour. Therefore, all the leaders and other key people in our organizations need to have the practical knowledge and tools to be builders of superior teamwork and superior work teams. I have written this book to provide them with that knowledge and at least some of those tools.

As has been the case with the earlier books I have published, I am indebted to my wife, Stella, for her help in reading and editing the pages of this book as I wrote it and for helping me put the completed manuscript in order for the publisher.

Dennis Kinlaw

Introduction

New Zealand tried three times before it won the America's Cup. When it finally won the cup the self-styled way that the New Zealand group referred to itself was 'Team New Zealand'. The secret to success, according to design co-ordinator, Tom Schnackenberg, was teamwork. The crew who had to sail the boat were involved with the designers and builders at every step from conception to launch. There was no hierarchy of management. The boat was a product of input from every member of the team. The result was that a myriad of problems were solved quickly and many improvements made in the boats design and rigging. Time to test changes in sails and appendages was kept to a minimum. The crew sailed a boat that they truly felt was their own. What happened to the Kiwi team is symbolic of what has been happening throughout business and manufacturing organizations all over the world. Teams are making the difference to the competitive edge.

During the past ten years, teamwork and teams have become the overarching strategies and common factors in all sustained initiatives to improve performance. They have become central to total quality management, continuous process improvement, total customer service, re-engineering and all other improvement programmes – whatever their names. During the past five years, however, the emphasis on programmatic initiatives, with their special titles, has lessened in importance and the emphasis on teamwork and teams has increased in importance. In the past, teamwork and teams have often been positioned as sub-elements in some larger initiative. Now teams *are* the initiative. In the past we have had organizations in search of teams. Now we have teams in search of organizations. The success of teams has been incontrovertibly established. When teams have *apparently* failed, it has been because, although groups of individuals were organized and labelled as teams, they never, in fact, developed into teams and functioned as teams.

Over the years I have listened to, read and examined a very substantial number of improvement initiatives described by executives from various countries and from many different organizations. After these executives have outlined the special characteristics of their initiatives, they typically describe the substance or operating elements in their initiatives. What they finally get around to describing are their teams and the successes of their teams.

One way to gauge the growth and importance of teams is by the numbers of teams and the many ways that they are labelled. There are 'executive improvement teams', 'total quality management teams', 'process improvement teams', 'self-managed teams', 'self-directed teams', 'quality action teams', 'employee improvement teams', 'quality first teams', 'case teams', 'cross functional teams', 'production teams', and on and on. But the plethora of teams and the variations in the ways they are organized and named in no way conveys the kind of team-centred transformation that is going on in organizations. What is now happening is that organizations are not just forming and developing teams. They are changing themselves into team-centred organizations in which everyone is a member of one or more teams, everyone is expected to function as a team member of the total organization, and the main actions of planning, operating, assessing and improving are being accomplished through teams.

Today, every possible opportunity for team formation and development is being exploited. Where traditional organizational units, like management staffs, intact work groups, projects, committees and councils continue to exist, these are being developed into teams. Where specific improvement opportunities are identified, teams are organized to respond. When problems surface, teams are formed to resolve them. The movement towards team-centred organizations is, however, advancing rapidly beyond developing existing units into teams or organizing teams to respond to special needs and circumstances. More and more all the work of organizations is being designed for teams and teams are increasingly designing the entire work of the organization.

There is no traditional function like planning, research, product development, design, production, marketing and selling that is not being done more and more by teams. We live in a time in which the team-centred organization is becoming less the exception and more the norm. Some of the most dominant and successful companies in the world already function largely as team-centred organizations, for example, Caterpillar, Champion International, LTV Steel, Textronic, Digital Equipment Corporation, and Cummins Engine. There are many, many more companies that may not be fully team-centred, but which make extensive use of teamwork and teams, for example, Kodak, Texas Instruments, Boeing, Hewlett-Packard, and Motorola.

The catalogue of the successes of teams is too large and too substantial to be denied. Here are a few randomly selected examples of what teams can achieve:

- Boeing cut the number of engineering delays in building its new 777 passenger jet by more than half with its thorough-going team structure and use of engineering integrating teams.
- EG&G Florida reduced weekly hold over of uncompleted work packages in its machine shop by 50 per cent.
- Texas Instruments' Defense System and Electronics Group increased revenues per employee by 50 per cent over a four-year period.
- Motorola decreased rejects by 50 per cent and reduced late deliveries by 70 per cent.

- Sun Life Assurance Society PLC eliminated most middle management and reorganized once-isolated customer service representatives into teams that handle jobs from start to finish. The result: time to settle claims was cut nearly in half, while new business grew 45 per cent.
- Bord Na Mona, an Irish peat-harvesting company, increased employee output by nearly 100 per cent.
- Martin Marietta reduced paper required for each NASA Shuttle launch flow process by 80 per cent per mission.
- K Shoes Ltd, in the United Kingdom, decreased rejection rate from 5 000 parts per million to 250.

Teamwork, teams and the process of continuous improvement

The process of continuous improvement, which includes all the special programmatic initiatives like total quality management and re-engineering, rests upon a set of experienced-based principles which can only be made operational by teamwork and teams. Teams form the warp and woof of continuous improvement. An analysis of the role that teams have in continuous improvement produces the following conclusions.

First, actual improvement is a function of the *potential* to improve. The potential to improve depends primarily upon the capacity of organizations to:

- create, integrate and use new ideas, knowledge, and wisdom
- develop and use the competencies of people
- ensure that the most competent people have the most influence most of the time
- make the most efficient use of time, materials, equipment and other resources
- build commitment and ownership of each person for the total performance of the organization
- manage uncertainty and change.

The interactive association of people is the most powerful means that we know of to strengthen an organization's potential to perform such a set of functions, i.e., people functioning in teams. Improving the potential for improvement means increasing the quantity and quality of teams and teamwork throughout the entire organization from top to bottom.

Second, just as the potential to improve is a function of teams and teamwork, so also is the actual *implementation* of continuous improvement a function of teams and teamwork. People working as teams provide the best way to implement and manage improvement. They are the fount of ideas and innovations for such improvement. But they are more. They are the vehicle for implementing such improvement. It is only as people work in full consort to create total customer satisfaction (internal and external), to make work processes more efficient and reliable, and to enhance supplier performance that substantial, sustained improvement is achieved. A sole person or group of persons, no matter how expert, highly placed or influential, cannot implement continuous improvement. Implementing continuous improvement is fundamentally a team function and the result of team action.

Third, teams are more than the source for strengthening the potential for improvement and the vehicle for implementing improvement. Teams are the *organizing principle* for improvement. Work is done through processes that cannot be understood or improved as long as people are encouraged to think that they perform independent functions. The traditional organization chart does not describe how work is accomplished. Work is accomplished in the 'white spaces', i.e. through the processes that connect and integrate the functions of the boxes. The separation of work functions into neat categories and organizational units like research, production, marketing, sales and the like leads to suboptimization, organizational fiefdoms, conflict, abuse of resources and poor performance. Organizing companies into departments, offices, divisions, branches, sections, etc. does not reflect the way work is actually accomplished, i.e., by the process flow of input to output from one individual to the next and from one organizational unit to the next. Moreover, placing people in functional and staff boxes and encouraging them to think of themselves as separate entities does not support the imperative that we must make full use of everyone's competencies across all vertical and horizontal boundaries of the organization.

Continuous improvement obliges organizations to structure themselves so that people see themselves as performers in various processes and members of the teams responsible for these processes. In his letter to General Electric (GE) stockholders in 1990, Jack Welsh and his colleagues described GE as a 'boundaryless company' in which internal functions 'begin to blur'. Getting the job done becomes everyone's job. Satisfying customers becomes everyone's job. Teams and teamwork know no boundaries and are the practical way that GE and other companies are reducing the time it takes to respond to customers, to bring new products to market and to make the many kinds of changes required to stay competitive.

Fourth, it is clear that adversarial relationships within any organization are dysfunctional. However, adversarial relationships between a company and its suppliers and customers are also dysfunctional. Continuous improvement is best supported when the entire organization is bound together as a collaborating, co-operating unit, i.e., as one grand team. This grand team *includes* the organization *plus* all of its suppliers and all of its customers.

It has usually been clear in the private sector that adversarial relationships with external customers are a certain path to decline and failure. There is today, however, a growing demand by citizens that governmental and municipal agencies treat them like valued customers. We are recognizing that an 'arms length' relationship with suppliers impacts negatively on every organization's performance. Quality in process and output is impossible without quality in input. The one sure way to ensure quality of input is to include suppliers on the team.

Fifth, continuous improvement necessitates a profound and radical overhaul of an organization's culture. When we begin to articulate just what such an overhaul means, we find that it means making teamwork and teams dominant values of the organization. It means making everything about the organization fully supportive of teamwork and everything fully congruent with teamwork and teams.

William Scherkenbach (1988) in his book about W. Edwards Deming's 14 points captures something of the meaning of team in continuous improvement when he describes the process for achieving total quality as a 'customer-driven, team-fueled … approach'. This change to a team-centred, team-driven culture is evidenced when leaders begin to respond to such team-focused questions as:

- How can we elevate teamwork and team performance as primary values of the organization?
- How can we integrate team formation and development into our strategic planning process?
- How can our hiring, promoting, and other personnel practices be designed to use teams and encourage team development?
- How can our award systems focus on teams and acknowledge team performance?
- What physical changes in the structure of work spaces and the organization of work must be made to support team formation and development?

Continuous improvement ultimately results from a team-centred, team-driven change in the culture of organizations. This means that an organization's physical structures, all of its policies and all of its practices must be assessed, modified and made completely compatible with teamwork, team formation, team development and team performance. One change that team-centred continuous improvement demands is in the responsibilities and performance of managers and supervisors.

Work teams and the changing roles of managers and supervisors

The emphasis on teamwork and developing work teams is having far-reaching implications for changes in the traditional roles of managers and supervisors. M&M/Mars has opened a new plant in Waco, Texas, with self-managed teams. TRW has a plant in Lawrence, Kansas, in which supervision has been eliminated. At Ibis, producer of industrial enzymes, teams are largely autonomous. At Aetna Life self-managed teams take care of all the functions for processing claims. These teams are responsible for the traditional supervisory functions of hiring, work scheduling, overtime and performance evaluations. The Johnsonville Sausage Company has eliminated supervisors and organized their production around Pride Teams who are responsible for managing themselves. General Electric has organized almost 50 per cent of its workforce into self-managing teams, and expects to realize a 40 to 50 per cent improvement in productivity from these teams.

The many radical and far-reaching changes in the way organizations are being restructured into self-managed teams has dramatic implications for the roles and functions of managers and supervisors. Where the jobs of managers and supervisors are surviving, we can observe a shift:

- from managing by control to managing by commitment
- from individual motivation and output to team motivation and output
- from the traditional functions of planning, organizing, staffing, evaluating to the functions of coaching and facilitating.

All modern improvement initiatives have increased organizations' emphasis and commitment to teamwork and team development by orders of magnitude. Teamwork and team performance have been demonstrated to be the two consistent strategies to achieve continuous improvement in quality and maintain a competitive position. The movement towards teamwork has taken on the proportions of an avalanche roaring through national and international firms, and carrying most traditional resistances before it. Traditional distinctions between supervisors and employees, management and labour are being swept away. Where these distinctions still remain they account for many of the shortfalls in the performance of organizations.

In those organizations that are moving from traditional structures to team-centred structures, the change in leadership functions are being communicated, in part, by the way that traditional titles are being supplanted by titles which reflect more accurately new realities and new expectations of leaders and employees. Title changes do not, of course, necessarily herald substantive change, but they do communicate intention. Co-worker, partner, team member and associate are replacing 'employee' and 'subordinate'. Team leader, co-ordinator, coach and consultant are replacing 'manager' and 'supervisor'.

The challenges that organizations face to remain competitive are enormous. The competitive game is tough and it will, without question, get tougher. The organizations that are winning are those organizations which are using team development and teamwork to make the leaps in innovation, quality and efficiency that they must make – if they are to survive.

There is, then, a growing commitment to team development and teamwork by managers – stimulated to a large degree by continuous improvement initiatives. Team development is more and more being accepted as the key to regaining and keeping the quality and competitive edge. In superior teams the synergistic effect is apparent. One plus one, plus one equals far more than three. The closer knit a group becomes, the greater the dynamism it creates. The greater the commitment within a group to a set of common goals, the greater the likelihood that members of the group will make personal sacrifices to meet these goals.

The need for a practical model

I have proposed above that teamwork and teams are what transform the potential of organizations into superior results. But though there is a present and ever-growing commitment to developing teams and fostering teamwork on the part of managers and other key employees, their commitment is often not matched with the practical knowledge and skills for turning work groups and total organizations into superior teams.

Team development is not easy and it is not simple. Even under the best of conditions, team development can be a task of mind-boggling, back-breaking difficulty. Without a clear, functional, and empirically based model to guide us, we unnecessarily confound the task and make it all but impossible. Without such a model, we operate without a blueprint, and what we do becomes confused and contaminated with unsupported opinion and bias. Consider a recent experience of mine.

I was asked to design and implement a team development programme for a large architectural firm. After a preliminary analysis of the firm's readiness to begin a team development initiative, I catalogued the following conditions in the organization that were working *against* team development:

1   Each of the main organizational elements in the firm was set up to bill the others for internal services and the result was an enormous amount of internal competitiveness, distrust, and bickering over chargeable costs.
2   The firm had doubled in size in each of five successive years and undergone numerous organizational changes. Whatever informal network had existed at one time was now badly damaged and not working.
3   In the process of rapid growth, new professionals had been hired in at better rates than many of those who had been with the firm since it started. A great deal of resentment now existed among the older hands toward the new hires.
4   The firm had no strategic plan and people had little sense of long-term direction. Work groups and individuals had very disparate perceptions of what was important and what was not.
5   The founder still ran the organization and had developed an inner ring of confidants who operated from Mount Olympus and who had no interest in sharing their visions and power with the mere mortals who occupied lesser heights.

But the biggest impediment of all to initiating a team development process in this company was that no decision-maker in the company had a functional picture of team development. Try as I might, I was unable to develop a consensus about such a picture or model and I finally abandoned the project.

I have become deeply involved in understanding and improving work team development and performance. Much of my work has been in conjunction with assisting organizations in their continuous improvement initiatives. I have analysed work groups in a variety of ways and tried to discover the general functional characteristics of work groups that distinguish them from work teams. But above all, I have tried to discover what distinguishes *superior* work teams from other work teams.

The data that I have compiled from these many team-focused activities and interventions have led me to conclude the following:

1   Leaders and employees have experiences on work teams – especially superior work teams – that they describe as remarkably similar.
2   Leaders and employees rarely have an explicit model of team development and performance that describes clearly the functional characteristics of superior teams.
3   Consequent upon 2 above, leaders and employees, largely because they have no well-defined model, often cannot efficiently initiate a set of integrated strategies for developing teams capable of sustained superior performance.

Questions and answers

In order to initiate strategies of building and maintaining superior teams (both temporary teams as in special projects and permanent teams as in work groups), managers and other key personnel must have a model or picture of what superior teams are like. I have built a model of team development and performance that answers the following questions: (1) what are the characteristics of superior teams; and (2) what are the actions that people can take to build and maintain superior teams?

My sources for creating and validating a model of superior team development and performance have been:

- a five-year study of over 200 teams and interviews of over 2 000 members of teams in 25 different organizations
- responses from over 5 000 people who have used the materials in our Superior Team Development Workshops to improve their work teams and their performance
- data from over 3 000 teams which have been surveyed with my Superior Team Development Inventory
- data obtained from several hundred managers attending my two-day seminar, Practical Team Development for Managers
- a review of studies published in the past ten years on work groups and work teams.

Later chapters in this book will be devoted to describing in considerable length the Superior Team Development and Performance Model that was created from my original study conducted between 1985 and 1991 and validated by workshop data, interviews, and survey data from 1991 to 1997. The model will be used as the basis for describing the key elements that organizational leaders team leaders and team members can use to maximize their efforts to build superior teams.

Purposes and objectives of the book

The purposes of this book are to provide leaders and members of any organization with:

- a clear idea of the opportunities for forming and developing teams
- a set of steps that they can follow in building superior teams
- a functional model that they can use for developing superior teams
- a list of the specific strategies that must be employed to build organizational support for teams
- a number of practical tools for developing and maintaining superior teams.

I have written the book so that it can be used by people at

different organizational levels and with different responsibilities for teamwork and team development. Information in the book can be used:

- as a guide for executives and senior managers who have the responsibility of changing more traditional organizations into team-centred ones
- as a guide that anyone can use to develop any group into a superior team
- as a conceptual basis for consultants and trainers to use to equip others to build, support and maintain superior teams
- as a tool for teams that are assuming the responsibilities of self-management
- as an adjunct resource for participants involved in any team development programme.

This book provides information that can help organizations answer the three questions they face in making the full use of teams:

1 What basic information is needed to form and develop teams?
2 What are the opportunities for team formation and development?
3 What are the organizational strategies required to support and nurture superior teams?
4 How are specific teams developed into superior teams?

Organization of the book

This book is based on my own work and studies, but it also reflects and takes into account the studies published by others about teamwork and teams. Because this book is intended – above all else – to be used and applied to the task of team development, I have kept to a minimum the use of references in the text proper. You will find in the References and Resources section, however, a list of those studies referred to in the text, and ones which I believe will serve the reader well as additional resources for team formation and development.

Chapters and content

The chapters that follow are previewed below.

Chapter 1: The basics of team formation and development

Team development proceeds at two levels through an organization: (1) the general level of moving the entire organization toward team-centredness; and (2) the discrete or specific level of forming and developing teams. To work successfully at either of these levels requires that we base our efforts on an understanding of a few basic *concepts* like teamwork, team, superior team and team development. We also need to have at least a preliminary notion of the *opportunities* for forming and developing teams. In this chapter I give a precise meaning to these basic concepts.

Chapter 2: The opportunities for forming and developing teams

Anyone who has had any significant experience in helping organizations develop and use teams will testify to the fact that most organizations have not fully exploited the potential of teamwork and teams, and that most organizations miss many opportunities to strengthen their process of continuous improvement because they miss opportunities to nurture teamwork and use teams. This chapter explains why teams can improve total organizational performance, describes how teams are typically used and offers ways for determining the degree to which an organization has fully exploited the use of teamwork and teams.

Chapter 3: Organizational strategies for team development

For teamwork and teams to develop fully and reach the level of superior teamwork, superior teams and sustained superior performance, they must have the total and unambiguous support of the organization's leaders and the organization's systems. It is a primary responsibility of the leaders of the organization to create a supportive environment, a context for nurturing teams. This chapter describes the main strategies that leaders must initiate and manage in order to create this support and this context.

Chapter 4: Basic steps in developing superior teams

Superior team development, as a cognitive process, follows a logical sequence. This chapter defines and discusses these steps in developing superior teams: (1) make the decision and communicate the decision; (2) set, enforce and revise team norms; (3) set team performance goals and measures; (4) use Model for Superior Team Development and Performance as a guide; (5) assess and evaluate current levels of team development and performance; (6) plan specific development initiatives.

Chapter 5: The model for superior team development and performance

The characteristics that differentiate a superior work team from all other kinds of work groups fall into four categories: results, feelings, informal processes and leadership. This chapter offers a rationale for making these characteristics the practical basis for understanding and building superior work teams.

Chapter 6: Focusing on results

The functional difference between superior work teams and all other work units becomes most apparent when we compare the results that superior work teams produce with the results of other work units. This chapter explores in detail these results and describes their implications for superior work team development.

Chapter 7: Focusing on informal processes

Superior work teams have a number of effective and efficient processes for achieving superior results. These processes include: communicating and contacting, responding and adapting, influencing and improving, and appreciating and celebrating. These processes are discussed in this chapter and implications drawn for superior work team development and performance.

Chapter 8: Focusing on feelings

The members of superior work teams describe the way they have felt in distinctive and consistent terms. Certain kinds of environmental conditions are conducive to the emergence and growth of these feelings and certain conditions are not. This chapter describes these important feelings and how they are nurtured.

Chapter 9: Focusing on leadership

Most superior work teams develop and continue because of the kinds of leaders that they have. Leadership roles and functions in superior teams are very different from the traditional roles and functions of managers, supervisors and other work unit leaders. This chapter draws some fundamental distinctions between traditional leadership and superior team leadership and describes the roles, functions and behaviours required of superior leaders.

Conclusion

This chapter reviews the key points covered in the book and provides a useful summary.

Appendix: Tools for developing superior teams

The appendix contains three tools which have proven utility for helping teams develop into superior teams. The tools are: using the Model for Superior Team Development and Performance; using the Superior Team Development Inventory; and using the General Systems Model of Team Performance.

References and resources

Although references have been kept to a minimum throughout the book, I have wanted to ensure that all material that relates to the work of others was properly acknowledged. This section includes bibliographical information on citations in the text and also includes a number of additional sources which have either historical or practical value.

1 The basics of team formation and development

Forming and developing superior teams is not a simple or one-level activity. Moving a total organization, or significant sub-element in an organization, to becoming team-centred includes the following kinds of objectives and actions:

1 Clarifying what is meant and intended by the terms teamwork, team, superior team and team development.
2 Developing a preliminary notion of the opportunities for forming and developing teams.
3 Using a set of organizational strategies to support forming and developing teams.
4 Forming and developing individual teams.
5 Describing several tools for maintaining team development.

In this chapter I am going to address the first of these objectives. In the next chapter I will discuss the second objective, opportunities for forming and developing teams. The remaining three objectives are the subject of the rest of the book.

Teamwork

A year ago a consulting and training house contacted me about doing some team development for the organization. I asked a number of questions to try and clarify what my potential customer needed.

Q: How many teams already exist?
A: We don't have separate teams, we consider ourselves one big team.
Q: How many people are we talking about that are on this one big team?
A: Forty-five.
Q: What do you want to accomplish through team development?
A: We want to work closer together, make full use of everyone's abilities, avoid unnecessary overlap, things like that. We just feel we could do a better job if we were more of a team.

After much more discussion I finally suggested that it sounded as if it was improved teamwork that was my potential customer's interest, unless he wanted to look at ways to form teams for managing and conducting the business of the organization.

The point of relating this little incident is to emphasize that teamwork is something that all good teams do, but that teamwork denotes a general set of behaviours that are not limited to teams. Teams are specific entities which have very specific characteristics, like being small enough to meet, sharing performance goals and existing for some considerable duration.

Teamwork is a condition that may come and go. It requires no special structure, only an opportunity for two or more people to engage collaboratively and co-operatively in undertaking some task. Teamwork exists outside the boundaries of formally constituted groups or teams. It can exist within groups for a time and then disappear, just as it can exist between two people for a while and then disappear.

Teamwork may exist only for the time that it takes a group to perform some particular task and after the task is performed the need for teamwork no longer exists. Group members can have teamwork one moment and then be disjunctive and at odds with each other the next. People can rally around some purpose and co-operate to achieve it and then break up again and become very competitive and proprietary.

Teamwork has the same meaning as 'working as a team', or 'teaming up'. It may exist to a very small degree or to a very pronounced degree. It may be present for a time and then disappear. Its most common-sense meaning is that it represents what people do when they begin to act like a team. Teamwork is best understood as a set of behaviours which two or more people demonstrate when working on some common task or pursuing some common goal. When people listen carefully to each other, when they seek and take seriously each other's opinions, when they make use of each others' competencies and expertise, they are involved in teamwork.

Teamwork describes both *qualitative* and *functional* characteristics when two or more people *begin to act like a team*. The *qualitative* meaning of the term is apparent in such everyday expressions as: 'we worked closely together', 'we always helped each other', 'we were all focused on a common goal', 'it was a team effort, everyone contributed', and the like. The qualitative meaning of teamwork is that it describes two or more people who are closely knit around a common purpose, who work easily together, who exhibit a good bit of trust toward each other who respect each other and who have positive work relationships.

The *functional* meaning of teamwork is that it describes that condition in which no one person can produce a specified result or perform a specified task. Teamwork here means only that two or more people worked together and produced something that could not be achieved by one person alone. It does not describe how well they worked together, but only that they co-operated sufficiently to perform their work.

Teamwork can, theoretically, exist anywhere for some period of time. It can exist for a time in families, in school classes, among manufacturers and their clients, between marketing and production – even between management and labour. It is clearly to our collective advantage to help teamwork exist all the time in all our social groups – at work as well as church, school and home.

When I have asked people attending my seminars on teamwork and team development to describe what they mean by teamwork, I have received the following kinds of answers. Teamwork means:

- helping someone else succeed in some task or project
- offering to help before one is asked to help
- asking the opinion of others and making use of their competence
- keeping others informed about matters that affect them
- responding without qualification when one's help is asked
- acknowledging the contributions of others to one's own work or project
- working together without disruptive conflict
- keeping one's word and fulfilling one's commitments to others.

The various subdivisions within organizations too often exist like multiple fiefdoms, loosely tied federations or out-and-out enemies. Organizations probably have an unlimited opportunity for increasing or enhancing teamwork – and it is certainly to their competitive advantage to do so.

Teamwork does not describe some entity like a work group, or a work team or a superior work team. It describes certain qualities or functions that may exist in any group for some period of time. In work groups, teamwork may exist not at all or only sporadically. In work teams, teamwork exists most of the time. In superior work teams, teamwork is intense and persistent. It exists all of the time. It is a way of life.

By way of summary, then, I use teamwork throughout this book to describe:

- a highly desirable condition that can exist for any period of time – long or short – in any set of people
- he *qualitative* characteristics that can exist for any set of people, like being closely knit together around a common

purpose, working easily together and having positive work relationships

- *functional* characteristics of units that must work together and co-operate in order to produce some product or service that cannot be produced by a single person
- the multitude of actions, processes, feelings and results that distinguish work groups from work teams and work teams from super teams.

Team

One way to describe a work team is to distinguish it from a work group. We know that both teams and work groups are 'groups', but what is special about a work team?

Work group refers to that organizational unit which has traditionally formed the basic building block of organizational performance. These are the units where the work of individuals comes together to form services and products which are conveyed to some user within or without the organization. In the past these work groups have existed within the various divisions of an organization, such as administration, research and development, sales and production. Today these traditional work groups are often being replaced by various kinds of work teams, e.g., cross-functional teams and self-managed teams. Significant differences exist between work groups and work teams and these differences will become clear as we proceed through this chapter.

Typically, work groups have a single supervisor or lead. And it is usually the case that work groups do not exceed 30 employees. But work groups may exceed 30 employees and use various forms of leadership. What is distinctive about work groups is not their number of members or their form of leadership, but that they exist to perform a set of tasks which, in some way, are united to make a larger whole. In other words, work groups cannot be defined quantitatively by their number of members or their number of leaders. They can best be described functionally by what they produce.

Work groups are the lowest level in an organization at which some additive or integrative process occurs. Work groups are the operational demarcation in the processes of production at which individual performance is no longer the primary determinant of success.

In a wind tunnel test group there are many individuals who perform many separate and distinct tasks. There are sensor technicians, model fabricators, statisticians and engineers – just to name a few. Each person in the group has a number of individual tasks which he or she performs completely alone. What marks the group as a group, however, is that all tasks are subordinated to the final product of the group which is a technical report or research paper. All individual tasks through processes of addition and integration come together in a group product.

An automobile production line needs thousands of separate tasks to be completed by individual workers. But at various points individual tasks become part of a larger unit of production such as the engine, chassis, drive chain and body. There are within the production line a variety of distinguishable work groups. These are the units which mark the points at which individual performance becomes integrated into a larger unit of production.

The tasks of individuals in groups may be combined through processes that are *additive, integrative,* or *interactive* (Figure 1.1). Various combinations of these three processes can, of course, also occur.

Additive processes are illustrated by workers in the same group who each use the same equipment or machine (such as a stamp press or lathe) to produce the same product, such as backing plates, winch cheeks, cotter pins and the like. The group's output is not integrated into a larger whole. Individual outputs are simply added together and the sum becomes the group's output.

In the case of production line groups the processes are typically integrative. What is placed on a chassis of a vehicle at an early stage in the production flow is not just added. It is integrated into a developing whole in which all the parts become mutually interdependent.

For design groups, software groups, budget groups, procure-

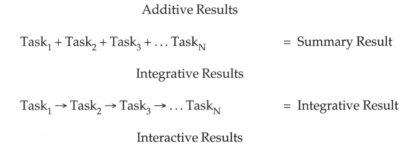

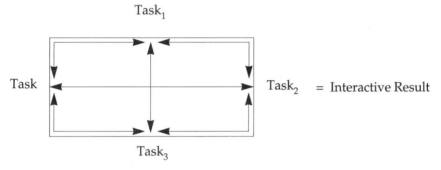

Figure 1.1: Work group task flows

ment groups, maintenance groups and the like, the end service or product does not result by simply adding together what each individual does. Their results do not occur through a process of linear (i.e., one way) integration. The process is interactive. There is a two-way flow of information and action between individuals by which the end product or service is produced.

The wind tunnel test group, referred to earlier, also represents an example of interaction. At various points, from conceiving a test to producing a technical report, the work of the test engineers, the model-builders, the statisticians and the like must all come together in a way that is not simply additive or integrative. The end product, a technical report, is produced by hundreds of steps which require interaction between two or more individuals.

A work group which uses only additive processes to produce a product or service may function without any teamwork.

Integrative and interactive processes, by their very nature, begin to force at least minimal levels of co-operation, i.e., teamwork. But, although work groups may have some degree of teamwork (required by integrative and interactive processes), they do not have the special characteristics of 'team' as I will be developing the meaning of that term and using it throughout this book.

Work *groups*, then, are units of two or more jobholders:

- which typically do not exceed 30 people
- whose leadership role is usually filled by one person
- in which the work of individual group members is performed through processes that are additive, integrative or interactive
- which are the primary unit of productivity in the organization.

Work *teams* are first of all work groups. But they are very much more. Teams have a number of quite specific characteristics, such as members:

- meet to make decisions, solve problems and practise at least a considerable degree of self-management
- share responsibility and authority for the team's performance
- share the leadership function
- work to achieve commonly held team goals
- have an intense identity with their team
- share in team recognition and awards
- make full use of each other's competencies
- fully involve each other in every aspect of the team's work
- regularly assess their team's performance and improve it
- are committed to the standard of teamwork.

Work teams must be of a size that permits team members to meet. Members must also share a common purpose, a common language, and have complementary skills. The difference between work groups and work teams, however, can only be described quite superficially if we focus on tasks or size or any such criteria. The differences between groups and teams are *qualitative* and *functional*.

The *functional* difference is apparent because work teams do things that work groups do not do. Members of work teams not only co-operate in all aspects of their task performance, they all share in what are traditionally thought of as management functions, e.g., share responsibilities for joint planning, organizing the team, setting performance goals, assessing the team's performance, developing their own strategies to manage change, securing their own resources and the like.

The *qualitative* difference is apparent because, even when work teams do what work groups do, they add value. For example, sharing of information is easier, issues are aired openly, and conflicts are resolved quickly and with positive results.

Consider the following contrasts. Work group A and work group B both perform the same kinds of tasks – say, home telephone installations. Both groups have members with the same levels of individual competencies. Work group A consistently outperforms work group B. What do we find when we try to account for the difference in performance?

We find that work group A:

- finds ways to take advantage of all the competencies of team members
- involves the whole team in making decisions about whatever affects the whole team
- meets regularly to keep everyone informed about changes in policy, workload, work equipment, personnel and the like
- regularly acknowledges and celebrates the achievements and contributions of its members
- makes it easy for members to make suggestions to improve the quality and efficiency of their jobs
- finds ways to enhance the competencies of all its members by sharing job experiences and information about ways to work more efficiently and effectively.

The members of group A and group B both perform the same kinds of jobs. They perform tasks which are *not* integrated or interactive to any significant degree. The difference in the performance between group A and group B results because group A is more like a team than group B – group A has *decided* to become a team. The sufficient cause for group A developing into a team has not been environment or the requirements of task performance. Team development has not been imposed. Team development has been chosen.

The point of this illustration is that a work group can take on the characteristics of a team just by deciding to be a team – even if this decision only applies to carrying out a specific set of functions. Any group of people can decide to be a *superior* team for any given period of time in order to carry out a set of functions.

Superior work teams

The larger part of this book is given over to a discussion of superior work teams. I would at this point, however, like to anticipate the following chapters and develop at least a preliminary definition of superior work teams.

The relationship between work groups and work teams and superior work teams should be understood as developmental. All organizational units that combine in some way the work of more than one person start out as work groups. Even when teams are specifically formed to conduct some aspect of the organization's work, these teams start out as groups.

Work groups, at least to some degree and for certain purposes, can develop into work teams. Work teams, at least to some degree and for certain purposes, can develop into superior work teams. Work teams belong to a higher level in the performance hierarchy than work groups. Superior work teams belong to a higher level in the performance hierarchy than work teams.

The more a work group is characterized by the following, the more that work group has become a work team:

- achieves certain distinctive results and sustained superior performance
- employs successfully certain kinds of informal work processes which support ease in communicating, making decisions, responding to change and improving

- develops in their members certain kinds of strong feelings like commitment, loyalty and trust
- develops shared leadership that focuses both on team development and team performance.

Superior work teams have the same functional and qualitative characteristics as work teams, but they have more. Superior work teams carry these characteristics to higher levels of development. Superior work teams achieve special levels of *consistency, intensity*, and *restless dissatisfaction*.

Consistency

When people describe their superior teams they use descriptors like 'always', and 'never'.

- 'We never failed to keep everyone informed about changes in the flow sequence.'
- 'Training never took a back seat to anything else. We always felt that if we didn't stay out in front on the learning curve, we would soon pay the price in new ideas and products.'

Superior teams are consistent in their pursuit of excellence. Quality is not a fad and teams do not live by slogans. They live by their constancy. They are in their jobs and their business for the long haul. A member of a design team reported this experience:

I remember once when our team was really up against it and we were beginning to break apart and talk about giving up. One of our technicians piped up and said: 'Maybe if we spent more time working the problem rather than trying to convince ourselves to give up, we'd get somewhere.'

Superior teams:

- *always* make maximum use of their people
- *always* achieve superior outputs against all odds
- *always* are improving every aspect of their business.

Figure 1.2 displays the relationship between work groups, work teams and superior work teams.

CHARACTERISTIC	WORK GROUPS	WORK TEAMS	SUPERIOR WORK TEAMS
Functional	Teamwork exists only as a specific task performance requires inte-grative or inter-active involvement of team members. No team manage-ment	Teamwork exists in most task performance processes and in most areas of team management	Teamwork exists in *all* task performance processes and in all areas of team management
Qualitative	Teamwork is rarely characterized by consistency, intensity and restless dissatisfaction	Teamwork is often characterized by consistency, intensity and restless dissatisfaction	Teamwork is *always* characterized by consistency, intensity, and restless dissatisfaction

Figure 1.2   Relationships of work groups, work teams and superior teams

Intensity

The level of energy and commitment is measurably higher in superior teams than it is in other work units. When you are in the midst of such a team you find people who are extremely impatient. They are impatient with:

● unsolved problems
● excuses
● irrational delays
● distractions
● poor preparation
● lack of focus
● trivia of any kind.

I have had some interesting experiences watching teams which have great intensity. Sometimes they develop a whole set of catch-phrases and symbols. During the meetings of one team, if a member started to say something and began with a long preamble, another member would interject, 'Don't dither, just go for it'. A project team posted its 'Top Ten', which were the ten problems that daily stood in the critical path of its PERT chart. Each morning 'top ten' badges were handed out to the technicians and engineers who had the responsibility to get the problem fixed. They wore these badges until they fixed the problem. What struck me about the badges was that they were not punitive. The badges signalled to everyone else in the project that the person wearing one was working a critical path problem and had a legitimate claim on any other project member for whatever that person needed.

In one of my seminars I remember a member of a manufacturing team describing his experience on his superior team:

When we committed to the idea that quality took precedence over everything – I mean like productivity and profit and everything else – we never turned back. I don't remember a single time of letting a job leave our shop that came back because of our work.

Restless dissatisfaction
When people have talked to me about their superior teams they have said things like:

- 'I remember all too well one poster on the wall: "If it ain't broke, improve it." '
- 'Everything was always fair game. Nothing was sacred. We could question how anything was being done any time.'

Some time ago while driving my young great-nephew to school, I was struck by the similarity of his behaviour to that of members of superior teams. Children and superior team members have one thing in common. They ask 'why?' and, what is more, they ask 'why?' all the time. Some work teams have so legitimated and institutionalized 'why' that they use 'Why Diagrams' in their team problem-solving sessions.

Superior teams are functionally and qualitatively different

from work teams. They are functionally different because members produce more superior results, manage more of their team's work processes and performance, and undertake more systematically the ongoing tasks of team development.

Superior work teams add qualitatively to the characteristics they share with teams by their consistency, intensity and restless dissatisfaction. In the following chapters I will develop in detail a model for superior team development and performance. The model describes what all work teams are like to some degree. But the model describes what superior teams are always like because of their consistency, intensity and restless dissatisfaction.

Team development

Team development and team-building are terms which are largely used interchangeably. This is unfortunate because, by doing so, we obscure some important differences and cannot fully understand team development. These distinctions can help us keep clearly before us what we are intending when we undertake the task of forming and developing teams. Figure 1.3 charts the following distinctions between team development and team-building that I believe we should make:

- Team development looks largely for positive opportunities to improve what may already be satisfactory. Team-building looks largely for problems in the way a team is functioning that threaten this function.
- Team development is continuous, long term and diffused. Team building is specific, short term and intense.
- Team development is proactive and focused on opportunities to improve total performance. Team-building is reactive and typically focuses on improving relationships among team members and the processes of interpersonal interaction.
- Team development is a proactive process that proceeds by predetermined design and is managed by team members. Team-building is a reactive intervention designed by an expert and managed by that expert.

TEAM-BUILDING	TEAM DEVELOPMENT
Deficit concentration on blocks to team's development and performance	Concentrates on positive opportunities for continuous development and improved performance
Short-term concern; emphasis on fixing immediate problems; usually intense	Long-term concern; diffuse, on-going improvement; part of day-to-day team work
Typically reactive; focuses on improving relationships among team members and the processes of interpersonal interaction	Proactive and focused on opportunities to avoid problems and ensure sustained superior development and performance

Figure 1.3   Relationships between team-building and team development

There is some overlap in the distinctions that I have made between team development and team-building, but the distinctions are real and can provide us with a good deal of guidance in undertaking the development of teams.

Team-building exists within the larger context of team development. For teams to become superior teams, team-building may never become necessary. Team development is always necessary. The more cognitive, planned, explicit and norm-driven team development is, the less likely it is that team-building will ever be necessary. If we maintain our automobiles properly we will have few, if any, breakdowns. Team development is similar to maintaining an automobile. If we do team development right, we can expect to avoid breakdowns and the need for team-building.

Positive opportunity
Team-building concentrates on deficits in team performance and its primary goal is remedial – to fix something that is seriously broken. Team development does not assume that something is wrong and should be fixed. Team development is the continuing and regularized process by which a team continues to improve

the way it does its work and the work it does. Some of the kinds of activities which are integral to team development are:

- setting and enforcing norms that govern the behaviour and performance of team members
- using a model of team development that defines tangibly the goals of team development
- assessing regularly how the team is working and how well it is doing its job
- measuring and improving the satisfaction of internal and external customers
- measuring and improving its work processes
- measuring and improving the input from its internal and external suppliers
- improving the interpersonal, technical and problem-solving skills of members
- discovering and using new tools to improve work effectiveness and efficiency.

Team-building begins with some perceived problem that is so significant that it must be resolved to ensure the team's capacity to function, proceeds through the steps of data-gathering, diagnosis, remedial planning, implementation and evaluation. Some of the more common problems that can require team-building are:

- Communication – people do not disclose what they know that could help each other; suggestions and ideas are not welcomed; hidden agendas abound; members do not treat each other with respect.
- Decision-making – people are regularly surprised by changes in their team relationships and responsibilities; members affected by these decisions are not consulted beforehand.
- Lack of disagreement and risk-taking – people play safe; people harbour unexpressed hostility.
- Criticism of people's motives and intentions – people are assumed not to really care, or to be inept, foolish, indifferent and the like.

- Open conflict – people fight to protect their domain; refuse to co-operate with each other; often use up energy just avoiding each other; go out of their way to create obstacles for each other; enjoy each other's failures.
- Members do not trust each other sufficiently to believe that members will consistently act in each other's best interest.
- Destructive competition – individuals and work groups perceive themselves to be in a win–lose contest with others; individual goals are pursued at the expense of corporate ones.
- Scapegoating and abdication of personal responsibility – people excuse and rationalize their own mistakes; people do not have ownership of the team's goals or decisions; a lot of energy is spent by people in protecting their own power and security.

If team-building is aimed at 'fixing something that is broken', then team development is aimed at 'keeping things from breaking', and 'making something better that isn't broken'.

Team-building is an important set of interventions in the continuing process of team development. Sometimes blocks to a team's performance do emerge that must be responded to immediately. Team-building encompasses a process and a whole set of strategies for doing just this. Team development, however, defines the process of continuous improvement that describes teams as they move from one development and performance plateau to the next higher one. Team-building concentrates on deficits. Team development concentrates on positive opportunities for even more effective performance. The relationship between team-building and team development is displayed in Figure 1.3.

Continuous and long term

Team-building is a specific intervention that is called for when a serious problem in the way team members work together has surfaced. Team-building invariably takes place with the team assembled and sets out to fix a problem like serious conflict, lack of trust, lack of demonstrated respect and feelings of being excluded. It takes place within a specific period of time. Team development describes the continuous and long-term process of making the team a better and better team. Team development is really a subset of the team's performance. Just as teams are always performing, they should be always developing.

Clearly the notions of positive opportunity, continuous and long term, are related. If team-building can be described as a form of treatment for ailing teams, then team development can be thought of as a team's design for continued good health and long life. Team development includes all deliberate day-to-day actions that a team uses to continue improving its potential for sustained superior performance.

A few years ago I was asked to consult with a financial group in Washington, DC. The presenting problems (just to name a few of the more obvious) were: 100 per cent turnover in staff during the past 18 months; virulent backbiting and criticism by employees of the firm's partners; open, injurious conflict between partners; scapegoating and fault-finding. The firm was clearly on the verge of breaking apart.

The first step, after a preliminary analysis and diagnosis of the problems, was to 'stop the bleeding'. I engaged in several team-building interventions just to get people in a frame of mind to work together and to begin the process of improvement. My first session was a weekend retreat for the two partners. The following Monday the partners had an all-hands meeting and publicly confronted some of the destructive ways that the two of them had been behaving. I continued the team-building sessions with the partners and embarked on regular team-building sessions with all employees.

Once the firm had been stabilized and people began to believe that improvement was possible, I began to put in place team development processes for the long haul. We did a number of things. With full participation of the partners and the employees we developed a strategic plan that explicitly identified teamwork as a dominant value of the firm. Until I began working with the firm, there was no systematic, explicit process of performance evaluation and reward. One of the next things that happened was that the employees, working as a team, developed an appraisal and reward system. The system was presented to the firm's partners and they approved it.

Team development is always integral to creating and maintaining work teams and for moving work teams to their next plateau of becoming superior work teams. Team-building is best thought of as a set of deficit focused, short-term actions. Team development should be thought of as including all actions which institutionalize the processes by which teams continue to become better and better.

Proactive by design and team managed

A final characteristic of team development is that it is a proactive process that is managed by team members. Team development is planned and rational. It is one element in a team's total performance. Just as a team sets goals for production and quality, it sets goals for its own development as a team. Just as a team measures its performance against production goals and quality goals, it measures its performance against its team development goals.

Team development is not something that teams undertake only as some special need or opportunity arises. Teams are developing, for better or worse, every time they meet, every time they work collaboratively to achieve a goal, every time they interact with each other, and every time they meet a new challenge or solve a problem.

Team development is best understood as a performance requirement. It proceeds in the same way that the steps of a project can be described and understood. Because team development can be made so explicit, it can and should be managed by team members.

The reasons that team development is sometimes not a self-managed process for which team members are held accountable are several:

1 Teams do not have a team development plan built upon a tangible model of what a superior team looks like.
2 Team development is not understood as simply one aspect of

a team's performance and integrated into the ongoing and routine functioning of the team.

3   Teams do not levy explicitly the requirement upon themselves to manage their continuous development as superior teams.

In this chapter I have described some of the ideas that are basic to the process of undertaking team formation and development. Successful team development and performance depends on every leader and every team member having a clear understanding of what they intend by such terms as teamwork, team, superior team and team development. These are the terms that I have discussed. In the next chapter I will describe another understanding that leaders must have in order to build team-centred organizations. They must understand the opportunities that exist for team formation and development.

2 Opportunities for forming and developing teams

In the introduction to this book I suggested that 'The movement towards teamwork has taken on the proportions of an avalanche roaring through national and international firms, and carrying most traditional resistances before it'. I stand firmly behind that statement and believe that organizations have no choice but to move towards a team-centred structure and to find more and more ways to employ teams to conduct every aspect of their business. Having said this, however, I must also affirm that even those organizations that seem fully committed to the use of teams have still not made the *full* use of teams. There are, certainly, very substantial costs involved in changing from traditional structures and traditional leadership behaviours to making more and more use of teams. The successes of teams, however, provide clear and unambiguous support for moving to a team-centred organization – regardless of the cost. Here is only a partial list of the kinds of instrumental and operational results that teams produce.

Instrumental Results (changes in attitude, perceptions and environments that support improved performance) produce:

- more interdisciplinary and macro focus
- heightened sense of personal importance
- improved communication
- flatter organization
- increased self-management
- less destructive competition
- greater and faster learning
- increased pride
- reduced suboptimization
- increased systems thinking
- greater freedom to act
- greater sharing of ideas
- improved job satisfaction and morale
- greater responsibility for final outcomes
- meetings that are more effective and efficient
- better decisions are made by developing more perspectives and options
- fair and equitable treatment
- improved labour-management relations.

Operational results (measurable outcomes in performance) produce:

- improved quality in services and products
- increased productivity
- reduced costs
- greater customer satisfaction
- greater work system reliability and efficiency
- better solutions to problems
- avoidance of task and project duplication
- reduced time from design to production
- increased market share
- reduced error
- reduced rework
- reduced work backlogs.

I am sure that the reader, in reviewing these lists of results, will think of many others. The positive results from teams are so varied and extensive that they are difficult to catalogue. We do not, however, need to develop exhaustive lists of the good results that teams produce. We have more than enough information to know that teams work and they are rising to ever higher levels of achievement.

Given the enormous amount of evidence that teams are an essential factor in the continuous improvement of organizational performance, the fact still exists that many organizations are not making full use of teams. There is one primary reason for this shortfall. They do not approach the task of identifying opportunities for team formation and development in a systematic way. The purpose of this chapter is to suggest such a systematic approach for identifying opportunities for team formation and development.

The uneven path that leads to continuous improvement and sustained superior performance winds its way through four main actions (Figure 2.1). All such actions can best be undertaken

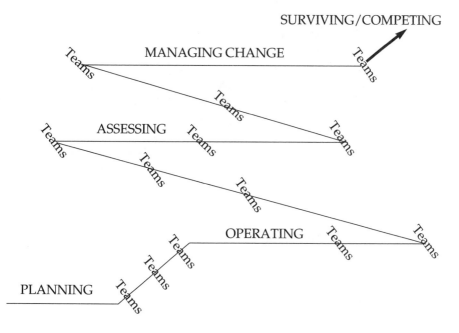

Figure 2.1   Opportunities for team formation and development

by teams: (1) planning, (2) operating and producing, (3) measuring and assessing, and (4) managing change. None of these actions is totally discrete. All of them at times will be the immediate concern of teams, regardless of the primary focus of these teams. I have listed these four actions separately in order to help us visualize what a comprehensive approach to the use of teams entails.

Planning

Teams will, of course, do their own planning for managing their own development and performance, i.e., planning performance and improvement goals, planning performance strategies, planning work schedules, planning special projects, planning for individual and team training and development, and the like. But teams are essential for undertaking the many planning initiatives of the larger organization.

An engineering design firm tripled its net profit before taxes and doubled its size over a three-year period as the result of using teams in most of its planning activities (*Journal of Management in Engineering*, October 1989). A state department of transportation dramatically improved its maintenance operation over a three-year period with a 24 per cent improvement in one fiscal year as a result of using teams in planning and managing maintenance (Output/Input: Department of Transportation Productivity Report, vol 1, no. 4, Pennsylvania Department of Transportation, Productivity Center, Transportation and Safety Building, Harrisburg, PA, 1985). In the H.J. Heinz company, teams were used to plan the shut-down of a traditional factory and the initiation of a new factory. The task was accomplished without any lost production time.

The planning process that should chart the total organization's intentions is strategic planning. In the next chapter, when I discuss the organizational context for team formation and development, I will show how teams can be used to accomplish all the tasks of strategic planning.

Operating and producing

Any action of an organization for operating systems or producing services or products presents an opportunity for team formation and development. Teams have proven themselves to be the most effective and efficient way to design new products, to manufacture products, to check the quality of products and services, to deliver products and services, to warehouse products and to respond to the needs of customers.

The Compaq Computer Corporation doubled the number of computers built within the same manufacturing space and increased by 50 per cent the number of computers built per employee by turning its traditional production line into teams of three persons which were responsible for end-to-end manufacturing of a main portion of each computer.

Asea Brown Boveri, an electrical systems and equipment manufacturer, employs more than 240 000 people worldwide and annual revenues of US $250 million. The organization is characterized by being global and local, big and small, with a radically decentralized structure and reporting and control systems. The company reports remarkable improvements in performance and credits this improvement to the company being organized into small work units and a multitude of teams. The entire company is run by an executive team composed of the four heads of product segments, the three heads of global regions, and the chief executive officer, who is based in Zurich. Operations and production are performed by a multitude of teams, small, cross-functional, time-focused and task-driven teams (Hall, Rosenthal and Wade, 1993).

A producer of carbon electrodes and various other carbon and graphite products uses teams to schedule and produce electrodes. Each team makes its own decision about the number of electrodes to produce based on daily consumption figures obtained from customers.

A small electronics firm in Colorado Springs, Colorado, USA uses teams of ten to 12 members for most production of its commercial video and special effects equipment. Most production is customized for its individual customers. Teams manage the functions of engineering, production, materials support and quality. Since 1989, this team-centred organization has shown an output increase of some 30 per cent with a workforce reduced by one-third of its original size.

Measuring and assessing

Measuring and assessing are the partners of continuous improvement. Measuring means assigning numbers to some performance variable like the stability of a work process, or the cycle time of some activity, or the satisfaction level of some customer. Assessing is the act of interpreting the meaning of the numbers. It is the act of making decisions to determine the adequacy, value or significance of a measurement. Measuring and assessing are the means for overcoming the great enemy of continuous improvement. They are the means for combating every form of data-free decision-making.

To picture the many opportunities for using teams to measure and assess performance, all we need to do is use a general systems model that defines the process from input to output in any organization (Figure 2.2).

These are the general categories for measuring and assessing performance that teams can address:

● customer satisfaction
● quality of output
● performance of work processes
● quality of input and performance of suppliers
● characteristics of the work environment.

To avoid any misunderstanding of the opportunities to use teams to measure and assess, I should like to remind the reader that every team is responsible for measuring and assessing its own performance, just as it must assume responsibilities in varying degrees for its own planning and its own operations and production. Teams, however, can be used to carry out each of these three actions for the larger organization. Teams will, of course,

WORK ENVIRONMENT

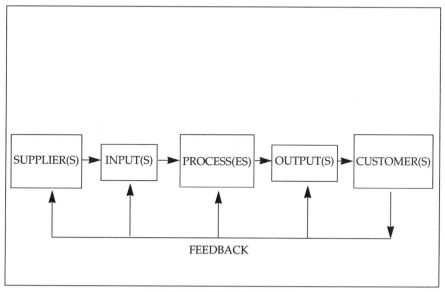

WORK ENVIRONMENT

Figure 2.2   General systems model

measure the satisfaction of their own customers, but teams can be
assigned to measure the satisfaction of all the customers of the
total organization or a major segment of the organization. Each
team should measure the performance of its own work processes,
but teams are the best possible way to measure and assess the
performance of some process or system that flows through the
total organization, like the procurement process, or some production process, or a design process. Teams are the best way to
measure and assess customer satisfaction, output, work
processes, input and supplier performance, and the work environment for the total organization.

Customer

All organizations and all subsets of all organizations have
customers. Every process and every operation in a process has a
customer. A customer is any individual, group or organization

that uses any output from an organization or a subelement in the organization. Internal customers are the ones within an organization which use some output from some other group. External customers are the ones outside the organization who pay for the services and products of the company. Here are two examples of how teams can be used to measure and assess the satisfaction of customers.

'Follow-up teams' can be used to visit and interview customers after the company has delivered some product or service. One organization that provides software for hospitals and other health care institutions routinely sends in a follow-up team to interview the people who are using the systems that have been installed. These visits are undertaken immediately after a system goes operational and then at six-month intervals for two years. Teams provide detailed reports that are reviewed by design, installation, and system training teams to find ways to continuously improve the performance of systems, documentation of systems and the way users are trained to use these systems.

A large government organization that I recently helped to change one of its personnel operations to a team-centred activity used teams to design and use several tools for measuring and assessing the satisfaction levels of all the people who were served in the organization by this function.

Customer needs are also made up of expectations, i.e., what they want in addition to what was advertised. Can the report also contain these additional data? Can the number of problem reports be reduced? Can the instrument be designed to power down automatically?

Outputs

Measuring customer satisfaction means measuring the perception and expectations of customers. Customer satisfaction is rarely determined by hard data on the cost, capability or reliability of some product. Outputs, on the other hand, can be measured against predetermined standards. A company may, for example, have a standard that all customer requests to be resupplied with some product will be completed within 24 hours. We can measure how good the company is in meeting this standard. But meeting this standard will tell us nothing about how satisfied customers are with the standard.

Outputs are in two kinds: services and products. These outputs can be tracked by many different measures, i.e., cycle time, performance against schedule, goal achievement, cost, errors, etc. All of these measures fall, however, into two general categories. Measures of *cost* and measures of *attributes*.

Measures of cost
The basic model for this kind of measure is:

$$\frac{\text{SERVICE OR PRODUCT UNIT}}{\text{SOURCES OF COST}}$$

Note should be made of the way the denominator is phrased. Rather than organizations considering 'costs', they should identify as many 'sources of costs' as possible. By identifying sources of cost, organizations will discover costs which they will otherwise overlook, for example, meetings, informal planning sessions, travel to inspection sites, preplanning time, time waiting for decisions, etc. Examples of measures of costs are:

$$\frac{\text{TIME TO PREPARE REPORT}}{\text{PERSONNEL COSTS}}$$

$$\frac{\text{NUMBER OF SOFTWARE CHANGES}}{\text{COST TO MODIFY PROGRAM, WRITE CODE, DEBUG}}$$

$$\frac{\text{PRODUCTION UNIT}}{\text{DIRECT AND OVERHEAD COSTS}}$$

Measures of attributes
The basic model for this measure is:

$$\frac{\text{INDICATORS OF ERROR, LOSS OR FAILURE}}{\text{SERVICE OR PRODUCT UNIT MEASURED}}$$

Measures of attributes compare an output with such things as error, loss or failure. Examples of attribute measures are:

$$\frac{\text{ACTUAL DAYS TO COMPLETE}}{\text{SCHEDULED DAYS TO COMPLETE}}$$

$$\frac{\text{MISTAKES IN WORK PACKAGES ISSUED}}{\text{WORK PACKAGES ISSUED}}$$

$$\frac{\text{NUMBER OF UNITS PRODUCED}}{\text{NUMBER OF UNITS REJECTED}}$$

Processes

A process is any sequence of events which begins with some input and delivers some output. A process contains the following steps: operations, transport, delay and inspection. Any process can be improved by eliminating steps, reducing time or reducing error.

Two measures that can help us improve a process are measures of stability and measures of capability. Measures of stability tell us how the process is actually performing. Measures of capability tell us if the process is able to perform within the technical specifications that we have established.

One of the most frequent uses made of teams is in process improvement. All large, successful organizations employ process improvement teams. Texas Instruments has employed process teams to redesign most of the traditional processes by which it designs and produces its electronics. By the use of process teams, Adolph Coors Company reduced by 50 per cent the time it now takes the company to develop and produce a new beer (Parker, 1991). H.J. Heinz Company used process teams to replace its multiple decentralized purchasing systems with a centralized one, and reported large savings in personnel, time and waste. The Goodyear Company has teams continuously looking at its key design and production processes.

The steps that teams follow in improving a work process are typically like these:

1 Identify candidate processes.
2 Select process or portion of process.
3 Chart the process.
4 Identify and eliminate redundancies and other non-value added elements.
5 Select measurements of process performance.
6 Develop baseline metrics.
7 Select improvement opportunities.
8 Make improvements.
9 Measure and compare to baseline.

Suppliers and inputs

The same variables for measuring customer satisfaction and input are applicable in measuring our satisfaction with our suppliers and their input. Quality assurance teams can set standards for the services and products purchased and then ensure that these standards are met. Teams can monitor the perception and expectations of the individuals and teams using the products and services of suppliers. Teams can benchmark services and products to establish a baseline of best practices for an organization's suppliers.

Work environment

Work environment influences performance. Appropriate variables that we can use to measure the work environment include measures of health, safety, and the perceptions and expectations of people.

Teams will, of course, always want to monitor the work environment of their own team. The Appendix sets out my Superior Team Development Inventory, which has proven to be a very useful way for teams to monitor their work environments and to improve these environments. But, as with all the opportunities to use teams described in this section, teams can be used to measure and assess the quality of the work environments of the larger organization. Measuring and tracking the quality of the work environment is an indirect measure of performance. If done correctly, however, it is possible to measure the perceptions and expectations of people in ways that predict performance. Measures of the work environment often produce results which lag behind more objective measures. In other words, these measures may tell us how the organization will perform in the future, even if they do not tell us directly how the organization is performing today. Here are some variables which we know predict the performance of any organization:

- *Clarity*: the degree to which organization members are clear about long-term goals, short-term priorities, roles and responsibilities.
- *Fairness*: the degree to which organization members feel that decisions about rewards, career development and resources are based on objective criteria.
- *Appreciation*: the degree to which organization members feel their worth and work are valued by the organization.
- *Responsiveness*: the degree to which organization members feel they get the personal and technical help they need in a timely way.
- *Influence*: the degree to which organization members feel they are encouraged to offer new ideas, can influence decisions and can participate in solving the problems that affect them and their work.
- *Resources*: the degree to which organization members feel that they have the time, information, equipment, facilities and people to do their best work.
- *Processes*: the degree to which organization members feel that work is planned and their work flow is logical, efficient, and effective.
- *Competencies*: the degree to which organization members believe that they and their colleagues have the knowledge, skill, experience and motivation for the organization to do its best work.
- *Improvement focus*: the degree to which organization members have specific goals and initiatives to improve their total performance, i.e., customer satisfaction, work processes, supplier performance, etc.

- *Teamwork*: the degree to which organization members perceive that co-operation, being helpful, and being good team members are valued and expected behaviours.

I have been discussing the main set of actions that all organizations must accomplish to improve performance and remain competitive. These actions are: (1) planning, (2) operating and producing, (3) measuring and assessing, and (4) managing change. All of these actions present us with opportunities for using teams. Thus far, I have described how teams can be employed to accomplish the first three of these sets of actions. It remains to describe the fourth.

Managing change

The best way to manage change is through teams of people with diverse capabilities, experiences and concerns; and then to connect these teams into a fully integrated, closely knit network. Figure 2.3 suggests a general team-based structure for managing change of any kind. In the next chapter, I will show how teams are used to manage the change from a traditional organization to a team-centred one.

Conclusion

In this chapter I have covered the basics of team formation and have focused on two tasks:

1   Clarifying what is meant and intended by the terms teamwork, team, superior team and team development.
2   Developing at least a preliminary notion of the opportunities for forming and developing teams.

What I have conveyed in this chapter is that leaders who set out to lead their organizations toward a more team-centred structure must have in mind a clear meaning of what teamwork and teams

TEAM	MEMBERSHIP	FUNCTIONS	KEY RELATIONSHIPS
Central steering team	Leaders from top management and unions	Authorizes the change. Integrates the change into the strategic plan. Obtains input from major customers. Prepares total organization for change	Interacts regularly with design team for co-ordination of change effort, managing major problems. Available to representatives from all the teams in the network
Design team	Representatives from major organizational functions, union members and persons with special competencies	Investigates best practices for similar changes, plans and schedules change strategy, designs support systems, designs the implementation teams and the rest of the team network	Interacts with steering team and the implementation teams to design the team network. Available to representatives from all teams in the network
Implementation teams	Organized by logical areas or breakdowns, like plants or geographical areas	Work with design team to plan and undertake the change. Each implementation team maintains active links with all other implementation teams	Work closely with design teams and all other implementation teams. Available to representatives from all teams in the network
Work teams	Operating and production teams composed of salaried employees and union members with competencies to perform work tasks. May be self-managed	Produce the services and products used by company's customers. Work in the new ways dictated by the change	Maintain links with all teams with whom it co-operates and all internal and external customers and appropriate levels of management and supervision
Special teams	Composed of anyone who is affected by a change or has the special competencies to help undertake a change	Undertake special change tasks like solving problems, testing new procedures, improving work processes, designing new products and services	Maintain links with work teams, appropriate levels of management and supervision

Figure 2.3   Structure for team-managed change

are in practice. Teamwork and teams exist in actual practice only when they produce results which cannot be produced by individuals or traditional work groups, and team-centred organizations consistently produce better results than those produced by more traditional, hierarchical, and functionally structured organizations. As better results are achieved by better teamwork and teams, superior results are achieved by superior teamwork and superior teams. Leaders cannot move their organizations towards team structures of superior teams without clarity about teamwork, teams, team development and superior teams.

I have also conveyed in this chapter that leaders cannot make the most of team formation and development unless they keep before them a general notion of the opportunities that exist. The main actions that organizations must take in order to move toward continuous improvement and maintain their competitive position are: (1) planning, (2) operating and producing, (3) measuring and assessing, and (4) managing change. I have shown how teams can perform these actions and given a variety of examples from various successful companies.

In the next chapter I will describe the organizational context for team development. Once that subject is covered, the remainder of the book will be devoted to the specific actions for developing and maintaining superior teams.

3 Organizational strategies for team development

Teams, the specific sets of individuals yoked together to reach a common goal, are a multitude of small organizations existing and interacting with each other, within larger and larger organizations. Team-centred organizations are messy. They do not have the neat lines of responsibility and relationships defined by the boxes of traditional organizations. Figure 3.1, graphically displays what a team-centred organization looks like. Team-centred organizations are characterized by:

- the interrelatedness of every team with each other and the total organization
- fluidity of relationships and movement among teams to accomplish immediate and specific goals
- leadership provided by management and executive teams
- the entire organization teaming up with customers and vendors.

Team-centred organizations are built by teams engaged in a process of discovery. No one can know at the outset of moving towards a team-centred organization, all the teams that will be

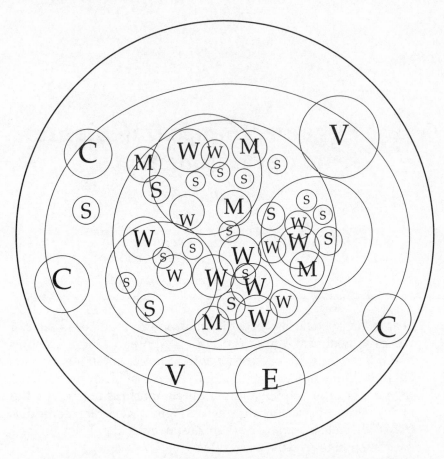

W = Work teams, S = Special teams, M= Management teams, E = Executive team,
C = Customer teams, V = Vendor or supplier teams

Figure 3.1   Team-centred organization

created, the new opportunities that will be discovered, the problems that will be encountered, the relationship among teams, or
how the whole team structure will be integrated and managed.
This does not mean that moving to a team-centred organization
cannot be planned and implemented in a deliberate and rational
way – like any planned change. But for teamwork and teams to
develop fully and reach the level of superior teamwork, superior

teams and sustained superior performance, they must have the total and unambiguous support of the organization's leaders and the organization's systems. It is a primary responsibility of the leaders of the organization to create a supportive environment, a context for nurturing teams.

We have plenty of evidence that teams do not live up to expectations, and too often fail completely. This evidence is sufficiently accurate, but the way it is interpreted is typically inaccurate. The common wisdom is that teams fail because of the performance of team members, i.e., they were not trained well enough or there was a poor psychological fit among members.

Behind most team failures, if we look deep enough, we will not uncover some inadequacy of team members. We will find some inadequacy in organizational support. We will find shortfalls in executive commitment, personnel systems organized for individuals and in conflict with team formation and performance, and a variety of other organizational factors that are in conflict with the idea of team.

As with any other characteristic of an organization, teams cannot be sustained unless they exist comfortably within the values, practices, policies and systems of the total organization. Teams can only be sustained by organizational strategies.

The meaning of organizational strategies

I use the term 'organizational strategies for team development' to convey the following:

- a planned set of actions
- which concentrate on the total organization
- which make teamwork and team development a consideration in all planning and decision-making actions at every organizational level
- which unambiguously establish teams as the fundamental unit of performance.

The strategies that I will cover in this chapter include:

1 Team-centred planning for the team-centred organization.
2 Team-centred leadership.
3 Team-centred organizational surveys.
4 Team-centred training.
5 Team-centred personnel practices.
6 Team-centred awards and appreciation.
7 Team-centred performance appraisal.
8 Team-centred environment.

Team-centred planning for the team-centred organization

A team-centred organization can only be built by teams. At the very heart of moving to team centredness is that this entire movement is planned and managed as a team effort by teams. If we apply the outline of team-managed change in Figure 2.3 to the task of team formation and development we generate the following set of responsibilities for the teams in the process.

Central steering team

- Develops and communicates to the organization outcomes to be achieved by moving to a team-centred structure.
- Communicates implications of the change and expectations regarding leadership performance.
- Integrates the goals of team development into company's strategic plan.
- Undergoes a process of team development for itself.
- Organizes the design team and sets its start-up responsibilities.

Design Team

- Defines the meaning of team and the levels of team development that are intended.

- Designs process, structure and schedule for team development.
- Identifies the specific targets for team formation and development, i.e., implementation teams, work teams and special teams.
- Arranges for resources with central steering team and their allocation to implementation teams.
- Identifies training requirements and plans training.
- Identifies the system changes that must be made and the strategies for organizational support that must be implemented: for example, changes from individual reward system to team reward system; changes in leadership expectations, training and development; changes in personnel practices; and the like.

Implementation teams

- Form the teams targeted by the design team.
- Deliver the training required for work teams and special teams.
- Provide coaching and problem-solving assistance to work and special teams.
- Provide the communication and leadership link among all implementation teams and among all work and special teams in its area or responsibility.
- Evaluate and assess process of team formation and development for design team and central steering team.

Work teams

- Achieve performance goals.
- Undertake training and development towards becoming superior teams.
- Maintain close ties with other work and special teams.
- Plan and undertake the process of continuous performance improvement.
- Provide implementation teams and design team feedback on progress and lessons learned.

Special teams

- Achieve special assigned goals, for example, benchmarking of best team training and development practices, assessing and evaluating organization's levels of team development, designing required changes in company's human resource systems, and the like.
- Undertake training and development towards becoming superior teams.
- Maintain close ties with other work and special teams.
- Plan and undertake the process of continuous performance improvement.
- Provide implementation teams and design team feedback on progress and lessons learned.

One of the most important tasks of the design team in moving an organization towards a team-centred structure is to define the levels of team development that are intended for each work team and special team included in its plan for team formation development. One of the greatest sources of confusion in forming and developing teams is that teams do not know how much authority and power they are expected to have. My own analysis of what organizations intend for their teams has identified the following three levels. These three levels are not an exhaustive breakdown of all the possibilities, but I think they can be used to help clarify what sort of teams an organization intends to create. It is possible, of course, to design a process of team development that begins by organizing teams at the first level and then moving these teams to the second and third levels.

- *Level one: consultative/dependent teams.* These are teams which may already exist as intact work teams or which may be newly formed teams. These teams have a supervisor who remains in control, but who delegates various responsibilities to the work group. These responsibilities will range from making recommendations to the supervisor who makes the actual decision to making decisions without supervisory approval. These teams parallel the traditional process of delegation. In this case, however, it is the work group functioning as a team which is delegated. At this level we have the traditional control model of supervisory control coupled with team development and performance. Job categories remain unchanged.

- *Level two: collaborative/interdependent teams.* These are also teams which may already exist as intact work teams or which may be newly formed teams. In these teams the role of the supervisor undergoes a significant change. All performance decisions are made by the supervisor in consultation with the team. The team is fully involved with the supervisor in setting performance goals, undertaking improvement initiatives and making all decisions that affect how the team functions. The supervisor functions as a team member. Most decisions are made by consensus. Team members are able to conduct all routine business without consultation with the supervisor. Final control of performance, however, still rests with the supervisor. Job categories may or may not be changed.
- *Level three: self-directed teams.* These are newly formed teams that replace the traditional functional structure in organizations. Teams are given end-to-end responsibility for delivering quality service and products to their customers. These are teams which operate without direct supervision. In these teams the role of the supervisor undergoes a radical change. There may or may not be an actual team supervisor. If there is a supervisor, he or she functions largely as a member and is held collectively responsible with other members for the team's performance. Job categories become few and broadly described.

Team-centred leadership

The behaviour of managers and other leaders provides the cues by which people in organizations answer the practical questions that guide their performance. Questions like: What are the real organizational values? What really matters? What is rewarded? What management pronouncements do we take seriously?

When people in organizations are challenged to be team members they naturally look at their executives, managers and other leaders to see what they are doing. Are they spending time to develop their management teams? Do they involve others as much as possible in their planning and decision-making? Do they demonstrate their valuing of the team leadership of others? Do they have their own team goals?

A key organizational strategy for team development is clearly that managers and executives must lead through teams and become models for team development. They must agree on what messages about team development they want to communicate to their organization and they must be living examples of these messages, i.e., must 'walk the talk'.

Team-centred strategic planning

Strategic planning is the continuing process by which organizations clarify and communicate what they are, what they do and what they want to become. Strategic planning further clarifies and articulates just how an organization will focus its energies and resources to achieve its strategic goals. Strategic planning should lead an organization to state unambiguously its core values, its few most critical goals and the strategies by which it will pursue these goals.

There are two main ways by which strategic planning can become a strategy to support the team-centred organization. First, it can give general and prominent visibility to an organization's commitment to teams and team development by including team development goals with its other critical goals about market share or new products and the like. Second, the process of strategic planning can be a team-centred activity. The process or shape that strategic planning takes can be more important as an organizational strategy for team development than the actual content of a plan. The plan, itself, can become a product of the total organization working as a team. A partial list of these activities includes:

- *Outlook.* Using teams to identify changes that will affect markets, products and services.
- *Competitive assessment.* Using teams to assess the strengths, strategies and market performance of competitors.
- *Benchmarking.* Using teams to identify the best practices of similar organizations.
- *Internal assessment.* Using teams to assess the operating, technical expertise, environmental strengths and weaknesses of the company.
- *Visioning.* Using teams to set the general direction of the enterprise and state what the primary self-definition of the company is.
- *Strategic goals and strategies.* Using teams to set those few, most important goals and strategies which focus the company's performance and which have priority for the company's resources over the next one to five years.

Team-centred organizational surveys

Organizational surveys can be designed to be powerful organizational strategies for team development. Surveys can be much more than ways of returning information to decision-makers in an organization.

Surveys can stimulate and support team development:

- through the process by which they are designed and implemented
- in their content and the variables they measure
- in the way that the organization is prepared to receive and use the results of a survey
- in the way the survey is followed up.

Team-centred organizational surveys use organizational units, not individuals, as the subjects of the survey. Each unit reports on itself. The data are fed back to each organizational unit, which becomes responsible for using the data.

Team centred training

The potential of training as an organizational strategy for team development is often only partially realized. Most training is aimed at helping people to: (1) gain the skills they require to lead teams, to work as team members and to facilitate team meetings; and (2) develop the understanding to manage their ongoing and continuous development as teams.

But when all training is team centred, then all training is team development training, regardless of the subject or topic. The way that training is planned and delivered can itself become a significant organizational strategy for team development, no matter what is being taught. When training becomes truly team centred we will find that:

- extensive use of teams and teamwork is made at every step in designing a training programme
- the target units of training are teams and not individuals
- the follow-up and evaluation of training is concentrated on team application and results rather than individual application and results.

Team-centred personnel selection

The selection of people into an organization and their subsequent selection for promotion has been traditionally based on two assumptions: (1) that a person will perform a job and have control over the results of that job; and (2) that a person works for some other person or persons. These two traditional assumptions are both erroneous, and the selection process that they have produced is, inevitably, flawed and inadequate.

Most people do not have jobs for which they, alone, are responsible for the results. These results are created though the integrated efforts of a number of people. Individuals are not the main unit of performance, groups of people are. Also, performance is not significantly tied to how a person works *for* another person, but how a person works *with* other people. The key issue, then, in employment and promotion is not how fit a person is viewed to be by a supervisor or manager, but how fit the person is viewed to be by all the persons with whom he or she will work – including, of course, supervisors and managers.

Selection can and should become team centred. When it does, it will have at least three characteristics:

1   It will include fitness as a team member and team leader as critical criteria for selection.
2   The team with whom the prospect will work will conduct the interviewing process.
3   The team will have the final authority to accept or reject the prospect.

Team-centred awards and appreciation

One of the clearest causal connections that can be demonstrated between performance and some other variable is between performance and appreciation. Organizations can expect to get the performance they reward.

Currently, the reward systems (both formal and informal) in most organizations emphasize individual performance. These systems tend to work against team development and inhibit teamwork by:

- overly emphasizing the role and value of the individual
- overtly and covertly encouraging destructive competition between individuals
- directing people's attention away from the task of becoming superior teams.

Team-centred reward and appreciation systems will have at least the following characteristics. They will:

- make teams and team performance the primary targets for reward
- make the most prestigious rewards for performance team rewards

- place the entire management of the reward system into the hands of teams.

A recent survey of 214 manufacturing companies in the USA and Canada, designed to capture information about teams, found that the companies in the survey were still struggling with the problem of designing team-based reward systems (Ellis and Tonkin, 1995). The researchers concluded that most companies are trying alternative reward systems that balance individual rewards with team rewards and monetary rewards with other kinds of incentives. Few of the respondents to the survey doubted, however, the necessity of building a strong linkage between team performance and pay.

Team-centred performance appraisal

As teams are more and more identified as the primary units of performance and production, it makes less and less sense to continue to use a performance appraisal system that assesses individual performance. The key characteristics of team-centred performance appraisal systems are systems that:

- emphasize team players as a key performance variable
- include 360-degree feedback to assess performance as team players
- tie individual performance to the performance of their teams.

Team-centred environment

A final organizational strategy for team development is using the work environment to reflect a commitment to teamwork and team performance. At least two characteristics of the work environment must be changed to support unambiguously a commitment to teams. First, individuals must have easy and free access to each other. Environments designed for team development and performance will be open and designed to accommodate the needs of teams to meet whenever they want without queuing up for conference rooms. Work spaces must be designed for team performance (Johansen, 1996). Easy and free access to each other means that little emphasis is placed on titles and formal relationships. It also means that symbols which emphasize levels of importance are removed, for example, symbols like 'suits' and 'non-suits', 'supervisors and subordinates'. It means no reserved parking places and no special cafeterias. It means that policies are written jointly by employees and managers, and that employees review managers' performance and vice versa (Shonk, 1992).

Developing groups of people into teams is a necessary step in building a team-centred organization, but forming and developing teams cannot stand alone. Individual teams must exist within an environment which nurtures and supports teams and teamwork. A total organizational initiative is required, one which includes the kinds of organizational strategies described in this chapter.

In the next chapter, I will describe the specific steps required in forming and developing individual teams, and in those chapters which follow, I will describe in further detail certain of these steps.

4 Basic steps in developing superior teams

Team formation and development depends on two parallel initiatives: (1) building the kind of organizational environment which supports teams and teamwork; and (2) forming and developing individual teams. In the previous chapter, I described the strategies associated with the first initiative. In this chapter I will discuss the second initiative and outline the steps for team formation and development which individual teams can use to build themselves into superior teams. The underlying assumption is, of course, that the first initiative is being attended to and the organization is committed to team formation and development.

General characteristics of the steps

Team development includes all the activities that a team undertakes which improve its capacity to perform, i.e., produce services and products used by its internal or external customers. Everything that a team does is, of course, part of its performance. I use the term development only to emphasize what a team might be doing at some particular time that is intended to improve its potential to perform.

Development towards becoming a superior team can never take place separately from the other work that a team performs. For example, as we will see, the third step in the process of developing itself into a superior team is that the team defines its performance goals (products and services that it will deliver) and the measures that it will use as success criteria for these services and products.

The business of developing a team can best be undertaken when: (1) this development is clearly understood to be the responsibility of every team member; (2) the steps in the process of development are made quite explicit and concrete; (3) the team manages its own development by consensus; and (4) every step that the team takes in its process of development is evaluated. All four of these conditions are related and actually qualify every decision and action a team makes when planning and undertaking its own development. It is useful, however, to describe each separately, for purposes of emphasis.

A team responsibility

Every team that becomes a superior team is, to a quite high degree, a self-managed team. All superior teams are empowered to manage their own performance. Such teams are characterized by: (1) members having a variety of competencies; (2) members sharing a common commitment to the team's performance goals; (3) members being accountable for most operational decisions relating to the control of production, quality, cost, schedules, hiring, firing, maintenance and evaluation; (4) members being responsible for co-ordinating their efforts with other teams and the larger organization; and (5) members knowing how their efforts impact on the business and strategic goals of the total organization.

As I have already suggested, team development cannot be separated from team performance. Developing the team's capacity to function as a superior team is as much of a performance goal as the production of goods or the delivery of services. Working on the team's development into a superior team, means only that the team is working on this particular aspect of its performance, rather than working on other alternative performance areas such as improving customer satisfaction, or improving some work process, or improving the quality of the products or services they receive from their suppliers.

The steps for developing superior teams that are defined below are steps derived from my many years of experience in helping teams develop. These steps work, but they only work when teams have discussed them, understood them and agreed to commit to using them.

In the process of accepting full responsibility for using the steps outlined below, teams may very well modify these to meet their own needs. What is more important than the specific steps is the team's commitment to a set of steps that are well defined, tangible and explicit.

Steps are explicit

Total *responsibility* is only possible when total *clarity* exists about what is expected. Team members cannot assume responsibility for the development of their teams, until they know exactly what this means. Each member must be able to answer such questions as:

- Where are we going?
- How are we going to get there?
- Where are we now?

Using an explicit set of steps for team development permits team members to behave consciously and responsibly in managing the team's development. Once a team has agreed on the steps that it will follow, these steps should be published or posted in some way so that the team never forgets what the steps are. Keeping the steps visible permits the team to re-visit them and assess its own progress through the steps.

Teams that progress towards becoming superior teams will eventually find that they have 'outgrown' the basic steps of team development. Having decided to become a superior team, they may have become so fully integrated in the team's culture that continuing to refer to this step may be unnecessary. A similar situation may also occur in regard to team norms. Norms can become such a part of the team's routine way of functioning, that the team no longer needs to refer explicitly to them. In other words, there can come a point in a team's development when it has moved past the early stages in its development and it becomes a 'mature' team.

Figure 4.1 shows the result of a small-scale study that I conducted recently to answer the question: 'What is a mature team?' A mature team will likely go beyond the basic steps of development and identify new steps that lead to still greater team identity, to increased accountability of members or to greater capacity to be self-correcting (and, therefore, more independent and self-managing).

Consensus

The basic steps in superior team development are steps which every team member must commit to, use and hold every other team member responsible for using. For such shared responsibility and full commitment to team development to be achieved, all decisions relative to the steps in team development must be made by consensus.

Consensus is a term that is not always correctly understood. There are two reasons for this: (1) people often think that consensus means little more than individuals abandoning their own opinions and finding the path of least resistance or the lowest common denominator which can accommodate everyone's individual belief; or (2) people think of consensus as a result more than they do a process. The best example of both kinds of misunderstandings that I know of is a quote from a former European head of state. She described consensus in these words: 'To me, consensus seems to be the process of abandoning all beliefs, principles, values and policies. So it is something in which no one believes and to which no one objects' (Healy, 1989).

Consensus is an interactive process which has as its goal:

MATURE TEAM CHARACTERISTIC	SURVEY INPUT
Performance	Consistently meets or exceeds goals
	Demonstrates knowledge of the company's business and ties its performance to the company's success
	Knows the difference between developing itself and working on other performance areas
	Continuously improves its work processes and quality of output
	Stays focused on satisfying internal and external customers
Identity	Every team member has primary work identity as a team member
	Manages own appraisal of individual and team performance
Flexible	Does not get thrown off track by planned or unplanned change
	Abandons dead-end approaches before it gets bogged down in them
	Changes direction easily when priorities change

MATURE TEAM CHARACTERISTIC	SURVEY INPUT
Accountability	Team is held accountable by its own internal and external customers and by management
	Team establishes and enforces accountability among team members
Independence	Solves own problems and fully uses resources of all members
	Self-manages most team actions
	Maintains necessary skill mix among members
	Requires direction, but not management
	Little or no dependence on direct supervision
	Effectively and efficiently manages internal conflict
Self-correcting	Able to recognize and correct own inefficiencies
	Maintains current and reliable measures of own performance

Note: *Information provided by 50 consultants and managers

Figure 4.1 Characteristics of mature teams*

- making the best possible decision
- maximizing the participation of the people responsible for making the decision
- making a decision that minimizes divisions of participants into 'winners' and 'losers'
- ensuring that everyone's position and opinion has been fully explored and understood
- modifying opinions by facts and logic
- creating unqualified commitment to a decision of everyone involved in making the decision.

The process of reaching consensus is what ensures the quality of the result. Consensus can best be managed when the following steps in the process are made explicit to the people involved:

1   The process of consensus is discussed and team members have a clear understanding of how they are going to make a decision.
2   The team holds a full discussion of the subject about which a decision must be made.
3   The team identifies where there is agreement and disagreement. It is useful to place lists of areas of agreement and disagreement on a chart or wallboard so all members can see them.
4   Different opinions are reconciled by using such techniques as:
    - worse case scenario
    - pro and con list for each alternative
    - having members with one point of view state what they think the other points of view are to test understanding
    - ask those holding out what it would take for them to accept the majority decision
    - collect more data and further clarify alternatives.
5   Decisions are reviewed several times to ensure that they reflect the will of the team.

Continuously evaluate
At the centre of Figure 4.2 is 'Continuously evaluate'. In the

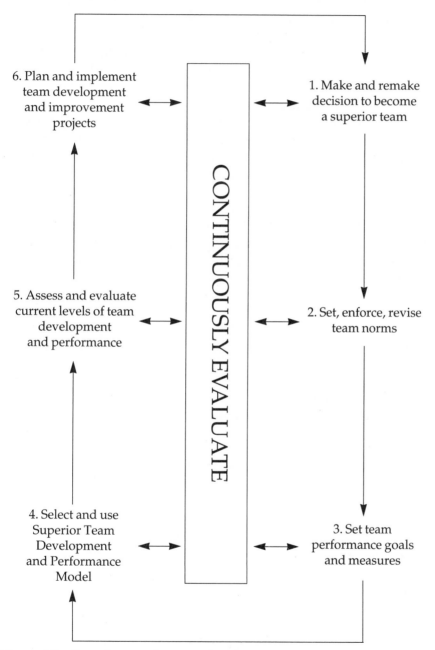

Figure 4.2   Steps in superior team development

process of becoming a superior team, nothing can be taken for granted and nothing can go unchallenged and untested. Continuous evaluation has at least two meanings: (1) teams assess how well they are doing compared to what they intended to do; and (2) teams assess if what they intended to do represents the best that they might intend.

A team begins its development by establishing norms for its meetings and for the way members will conduct all their business with each other. For norms to work, teams must regularly assess how well they are meeting the requirements of these norms, but teams must also assess the degree to which their norms are the very best and most demanding that they can invent. For teams to develop into superior teams, they must set challenging and compelling performance goals. They will regularly determine by their performance measures how well they are doing to reach these goals. But they will also regularly determine if their goals and measures represent what they believe they can achieve if they steadfastly do their best.

A team may put together an evaluation tool to assess how well its meetings are going. It may eventually find that it is meeting all the criteria that it has originally set for itself. Does it then stop evaluating its meetings? Certainly not. It looks for new opportunities to assess its meetings and improve them. It may begin to experiment with various kinds of interactive software (often called group ware) so that team members can interact without actually meeting and without sharing information at the same time. The use of electronic mail is a very simple example of this kind of possibility.

The basic steps for managing superior team development

The qualitative characteristics of the steps for managing superior team development are: (1) this development is clearly understood to be the responsibility of every team member; (2) the steps in the process of development are made quite explicit; (3) the team manages its own development by consensus; and (4) continuously evaluate. The specific steps that we can use to develop a superior team are:

1 Make and remake the decision to become a superior team.
2 Set, enforce and revise team norms.
3 Set team performance goals and measures.
4 Use the Model for Superior Team Development and Performance as a guide.
5 Assess and evaluate current levels of team development and performance.
6 Plan and implement team development and performance improvement projects.

I have called the sequence of team development 'steps', in order to emphasize that team development can be a cognitive, conscious and orderly activity. All these steps are, however, interactive and all steps and each step are continuously evaluated. Figure 4.2 displays the steps so that the ideas of interaction and continuous evaluation are emphasized.

Step 1: make and remake the decision to become a superior team

I have, throughout this book, placed great emphasis on the conscious and deliberate nature of team development. Team development can happen most efficiently and effectively when it happens by intention and design. The first step in becoming a superior team is to make the decision to become a superior team.

Commitment to becoming a superior team is, itself, a developmental process. It starts with a decision, but this decision must be reinforced over time and the decision must be revisited until such revisiting clearly becomes less and less necessary. We can tell when a potential team has decided that it wants to be a superior team and is committed to fulfilling the decision when we begin to observe that members routinely:

● volunteer for the more difficult team jobs
● subordinate their personal needs to the needs of the team

- describe themselves to others as the member of such and such team
- demand that they be held fully accountable for their responsibilities to the team.

At each subsequent step in developing itself, a team must test its resolve to be a superior team. The decision to become a superior team marks only the first step in an endless journey of becoming a better and better team. It is, however, a critical step. By making the conscious and explicit decision to become a superior team, the team has begun to define itself and to develop its special identity. Superior teams always have members who have a lively sense of their identity as a team, i.e., what makes their team special.

The decision to become a superior team must be reaffirmed and its meaning redefined as a team develops. Teams can only discover for themselves the exact dimensions of what 'superior' means to them as they proceed through each of the subsequent developmental steps. But as teams proceed through these steps they can look back over their shoulder to the moment at which they resolved to become superior, interpret what they are now doing in the light of that decision, and project how the decision will define their futures.

People become doctors, engineers, writers, priests, painters and poets because they *decide* to become one or another of these. People may back into various jobs by taking paths of least resistance, but qualifications in medicine and the arts come by decision followed by effort. So too with superior teams. Superior teams do not happen by chance. They are created by groups of people deciding that this is the future they want.

Step 2: set, enforce and revise team norms

Norms are the guides, rules, standards, or measuring stick that team members use to direct and judge the way they work together. Teams need two sets of norms. They need a set which governs the way they conduct their team meetings, and they need a set which describes the way they will conduct all of their team's work. The degree to which teams set useful norms, enforce and revise these norms will determine their success in carrying out all the other steps in developing themselves into superior teams.

Evidence for the need for explicit norms to govern the behaviour of groups can be found at every hand. This need goes far beyond teams. Every time I have become involved with groups or teams that were experiencing some problem in managing their performance, I discovered that one of the problems has been the lack of clear norms that were understood and enforced by members of these groups or teams.

The president of a religious congregation contacted me a few months ago and asked for my help with a problem that the congregation was having during its regular weekly meetings. During these meetings it was the custom for the presiding official to ask members to voice any 'concerns' or 'joys' that they wanted to share with their friends. Some members used the opportunity to complain about the way other members had carried out a responsibility, like organizing a congregational supper or caring for the grounds. Others actually used the opportunity to call attention to the apparent lack of skills, motivation or wisdom of other members. The result of turning their 'concerns' into an opportunity to criticize their colleagues was predictably inflammatory and divisive. After I had listened a while to the president of the congregation talk about the problem, I asked him: 'Does the congregation have a set of norms that it follows during its weekly meeting?' The answer was, predictably, 'No'.

My experience with this religious group mirrored an experience that I have had time and time again, when people have asked for my help with some group or team. What I eventually find out is that these groups and teams are trying to function *without* norms.

I was asked to facilitate an extended meeting for the senior directors of an aerospace firm some years ago. At the outset of the meeting I asked members to build a set of norms to clarify the way they would conduct the process of designing a strategic plan. The chief executive officer quickly indicated that they did not need norms, that they had all worked together for some time, and knew what to expect from each other.

We did not establish norms and the results were inevitable. The progress of the meeting was hindered by members periodically 'subgrouping' and carrying on private conversations while the general meeting was in progress, by members not knowing how decisions would be made, by individuals not having some idea about the time permitted for individual presentations, and a variety of other such problems.

Teams need one set of norms which will guide the way the team conducts its meetings. Norms for meetings are not 'rules of order'. They do not structure the interaction among members so severely that communication is formal or constricted and the energetic involvement of members is limited in any way.

Norms for team meetings answer such questions as: Will meetings start and stop at specific times? Will meetings start even if everyone is not present? Norms refer also to how the team will make its decisions. Will the team make decisions or only advise? Will decisions be made by consensus? By voting? Norms refer, finally, to how the team will interact. Is it an open, give and take meeting? Is open confrontation encouraged? How will conflict be managed? Is everyone responsible for ensuring that no one person monopolizes the team? The great value in taking time to establish clear and explicit norms is that the onus for enforcing timeliness, confronting people who tend to dominate and managing other similar dysfunctional behaviour, is removed from any one person's responsibility. The team becomes responsible and reference to the norms becomes a way of managing the team.

One of the traditional, and widely accepted, descriptions of the way teams develop suggests that teams go through four stages:

1 Forming
2 Storming
3 Norming
4 Performing.

This is a very unsatisfactory way of thinking about team development for several reasons:

1 It fails to emphasize that team development can be a

cognitive, conscious, deliberate undertaking in which these stages do not apply. It is not necessary for teams to go through a 'storming' phase if team members follow the steps that I am outlining.

2   It suggests that teams follow a set of nicely distinguishable phases, when in fact teams develop in stops and spurts. At any one time teams will be managing a conflict, i.e., 'storming'. At another time the team will be reviewing and modifying its guidelines and standards, i.e., 'norming'. At yet another time the team may be focusing on its goals and objectives, i.e., 'performing'.

3   The most serious problem with this model of team development is that it separates development from performance. It pictures a team developing itself and then undertaking to achieve its other goals. Such a dichotomy is a serious mistake and leads teams to consider development as 'not real work'. In fact the development of superior teams is only possible when such development is planned as a set of performance goals (like any other set of performance goals) and these are integrated into the team's total performance effort.

Norming is accomplished at the earliest possible moment of team development. Only by setting norms can the decision to become a superior team become operative in the team's life.

As I suggested above, teams need two sets of norms. They need one which governs the way meetings are managed. They need a second that governs how every aspect of the team's work will be accomplished. There will often be an overlap between these two sets. Meetings are work, but they are work for which all members need to be present. It therefore is qualitatively different from work that is accomplished through the routine interactions of one or more team members. Here is one example of meeting norms:

Administrative
●   Rotate leader/facilitator for each meeting.
●   Publish agenda at least 36 hours before meeting, except in emergencies.

- Everyone completes personal preparation and assigned work prior to meeting.
- Keep record of each meeting and publish summary to each member within 24 hours of meeting's end.
- Start and end all meetings on time.

Communication/interaction
- Stay focused on tasks and do not waste time.
- Listen to each other and take each other's ideas seriously.
- Do not criticize members, focus on facts, problems, opportunities.
- Never monopolize the conversation.
- Make all decisions by consensus, unless the team unanimously agrees to act otherwise.
- Make full use of everyone's competencies.

Here is an example of norms that might govern the way a team undertakes all of its work:

Customer
- Everything we provide our internal and external customers will be 100 per cent fit to use 100 per cent of the time.
- Ensure at all times that we know our customers' needs and expectations.

Involvement
- Fully use each other as resources.
- Involve each person affected by any action in that action.
- Respond willingly and quickly to any request for help from another team member.

Performance
- Set specific performance goals with measurable success criteria.
- Meet or exceed all performance goals.
- Continuously improve every aspect of our performance, including our development as a team.

Step 3: set team performance goals and measures

One of the most obvious characteristics of superior teams is that they have well-defined performance goals and measures. Early in its formative process a group that intends to become a superior team must set down for itself exactly what products or services it intends to produce and how its performance against these goals will be measured. This is an important developmental step.

Teams cannot develop without clarity of purpose and explicit performance criteria. Without such goals and measures, teams cannot develop into performance units. They will remain groups of individuals joined together for no clear reason, i.e., they will not share a set of common goals which can be achieved only by interaction and collaboration. Without such shared goals groups may look like teams, but they are really pseudo-teams. Superior teams always have performance goals and these goals have certain characteristics which are common to all superior teams. These characteristics are:

- Goals are team goals.
- Goals are challenging and compelling.
- Goals are tangible and communicable.
- Goals are measurable and attainable.

Goals are team goals
Team performance goals necessitate the full participation and contribution of every team member. Team goals can only be achieved by the team. These are not goals which are the summation of the contribution of individuals, like measuring the collective result of a group of workers picking apples, or counting how many procurement packages a group of workers issues separately, or adding the collective results of a group of mail carriers distributing mail, or adding up the total sales of a group of salespeople who operate independently of each other. Team goals concentrate on reducing cycle time, cutting costs, improving customer response time, bringing a new product to market and improving market share. Team goals define the purpose of a team in the same way that organizational goals define the purpose of the organization.

Goals are challenging and compelling

Team goals lead to the development of superior teams and superior performance when these goals are challenging and compelling. They are goals that carry a significant possibility of failure. When a project team commits to bringing a project in under cost and ahead of schedule, the team knows that its reputation and future are at stake. When a personnel team commits to cutting in half the time it takes to fill a job vacancy; a warehouse team commits to reducing inventory by 30 per cent, while reducing fulfilment time by 30 per cent; a human resources team commits to delivering cost-effectiveness ratios to measure value delivered by its training programmes; every team member knows that these are not trivial goals and that they will only be achieved if each member makes a strenuous effort and subordinates individual goals to the goals of the team.

Goals are tangible and communicable

Team identity is largely determined by having goals which are so tangible that they are easily communicated among team members and between the team and the rest of the organization. Team goals help team members make the day-to-day decisions about what is important and how to spend their efforts.

Clear team goals lead to a number of efficiencies. For example, such goals make it easy for teams to avoid wasting time at team meetings. They also make it a lot easier for team members to resolve conflicts when these arise. Conflicts which are not related to the achievement of goals are easily recognized as unproductive, and are discarded as not worth bothering about. Tangible team goals reinforce mutual interdependency and contribute directly to the team's continuous development into a better and better team. Just by aiming to achieve a specific goal, team members are forced to consider how the goal can be achieved. Common team goals that are tangible can be communicated. Team goals that can be communicated force teams to manage the achievement of these goals by functioning as teams. The more challenging and compelling the goals, the higher the levels of team development that are needed to achieve the goals.

Goals are measurable and attainable

Superior team development and the achievement of sustained superior performance are meaningless phrases until we are able to measure the team's success in achieving its goals. Measurement must be kept in tension with the notion of attainability. Superior teams are always teams that achieve superior results which are verifiable.

Teams often start out with what sound like goals, but which are really purposes. They are not specific enough to be measured. In a medium-sized electronics firm, teams assigned the job of cutting production costs soon developed specific measurable goals to:

- reduce rework to less than 1 per cent of output
- achieve on-time delivery to customers 97 per cent of the time
- reduce inventory costs by half.

A fabrication shop set up teams with designers to reduce the time that it took to produce a product after a design was received from the company's engineers. To enable these teams to obtain specific measurable outcomes, the teams set for themselves goals like:

- reduce changes to designs received by 75 per cent
- achieve zero modifications to products built
- reduce average time from receipt of design to finished product by 30 per cent.

Specific measurable goals are at the very heart of team development and the continuous improvement of team performance. Until teams have set challenging and compelling goals against which they can measure their performance, they can never become superior teams. To set the goal of improving some work process, i.e., to make it more efficient and reliable, requires the periodic measurement of one or more quality indicators over time. Achievement and improvement do not exist (in any useful way) until they are measured.

By developing and using measurable goals, teams keep concrete opportunities in mind. Measuring performance against goals will typically cause teams to identify new ways to achieve their goals, or even cause them to identify new performance goals.

A company that offers insurance and various other financial planning services and products organized itself into teams to provide total customer service. Each team managed the complete needs of a customer from the moment of initial contact, through the investment phase and on to continuous customer service. These teams started out by setting specific goals such as improving the on-time delivery of insurance policies. Their contacts with their customers, however, soon led to goals for improving the financial planning process the company had been using, increasing the number of follow-up contacts with customers, and for increasing the use of certain types of financial investment instruments.

Celebrating success has a causal relationship to performance. Feeling successful creates the desire to continue to feel successful. The best teams celebrate their success. It is difficult to celebrate achievements that cannot be measured. One of the great values in measurement that we sometimes overlook is precisely this – measurement permits teams to acknowledge achievement in a quite clear and unambiguous way.

Measurement creates involvement of team members in the goals of the team. Measurement provides the feedback that helps members take a more active role in improvement and to take more direct responsibility for it. When performance goals are vague and progress goes unmonitored, team members can easily remain on the sidelines and avoid ownership.

Step 4: select and use the Superior Team Development and Performance Model

In Chapter 1, in discussing the basics of team development, I suggested that team development is a difficult task at best, and one that becomes impossible without a clear, functional and empirically based model to guide leaders and team members. It remains the case, however, that one of the truly amazing behaviours of organizational leaders, team leaders and team members is that they will launch team formation and team development *without ever having clarified where they are going*, i.e., what are the characteristics of the teams they are forming and developing. A related problem is that, even when some effort is made to define the characteristics of team, this effort falls short of defining the characteristics of a *superior team*.

Some years ago I was involved in a large team-centred quality improvement training initiative for the National Aeronautics and Space Administration (NASA) in the USA. We trained some 6 500 people from NASA and its contractors in a two-day workshop. The biggest single obstacle of the entire effort was that senior managers in all the organizations involved had notions of what teams were that were too vague or just plain wrong. The picture of teams and teamwork that one chief executive officer held can be summarized as follows:

- I own the team and everyone is a member of the team by my good pleasure.
- I am the leader of the team, and good team members do what I say.
- Good team members keep their jobs on the team.

One of the most common misunderstandings of life in a team is that teams are free of serious disagreement and conflict. Superior teams are, in fact, places of great energy, of widely differing opinions and of considerable conflict. Superior teams are not marked by the absence of conflict, but how conflict is used and resolved.

Why use the Model for Superior Team Development and Performance?
There are a multitude of team development models. I have already drawn attention to the forming, storming, norming, performing model, but there are many others (cf. Gouillart and Kelly, 1995; Hensey, 1992; Katzenbach and Smith, 1993). The reason for putting forward my own Model for Superior Team Development and Performance is not that other models do not have value. Probably any attempt to picture what a team looks like has value. I propose that teams use my model for the following reasons:

1   It was derived for the purpose of identifying what *superior* teams look like, and not what *teams* (in some generic or general sense) look like.

2   It was derived from a very broad base of human experience, i.e., some 25 organizations, 200 teams, and 2000 interviews of team members.

3   Since the original study was conducted, the utility of the model has been proven over the course of five years in our work with several hundred teams in a wide variety of organizations.

4   It has proven its utility for new teams that are just starting up, as well as with quite mature teams which have been in place for years.

5   It has proven its utility for every kind of team, e.g., management teams, intact work teams, process improvement teams, project teams, problem-solving teams.

6   It has proven its applicability to teams in organizations from most areas of the public and private sector, e.g., health care, finance, government, manufacturing, engineering, business and the like.

7   It provides a clear basis for the continuous assessment of team development and performance that can be translated into specific team improvement projects.

How to use the model

The model provides the conceptual basis for understanding superior teams and it leads directly to ways for teams to self-manage their development and continuous performance as superior teams. Here is how the model can be used at the very beginning of the process of team formation and development, and throughout the life of the team:

1   Use the model to develop clarity about the team's goals for its own development, i.e. to become a superior team that has the characteristics outlined in the model.

2   Use the model to assess the team's level of development shortly after its formation and thereafter on a regular basis. The Superior Team Development Inventory (see the

Appendix), which is based on the model, can be used to assess a team's development, monitor its continuing development and provide a benchmark for comparing itself to other superior teams.

3   Use the model and the assessment process to identify and undertake specific projects to develop the team and improve its performance.

Step 5: assess and evaluate current levels of team development and performance

Continuous improvement for a team, as with any other person or group, is only possible through regular and systematic assessment. There are many opportunities and many ways for a team to assess and evaluate its current levels of team development and performance. Here are three such opportunities:

- performance management
- critical characteristics
- team meetings.

Performance management

A team is responsible for managing its total performance. One way to understand just what comprises total performance is by referring to the General Systems Model of Team Performance. A copy of the model is found in Figure 4.3. A full description of how to use the model is also found in the Appendix.

This model identifies the main areas of development and performance which are involved in managing the team's total life and work. The team occupies three roles. Sometimes it is a supplier and looks at the needs of its customers. Sometimes it is a processor and looks at the work sequences by which it produces its various outputs. Sometimes it is a customer and looks at its suppliers and the output of its suppliers. The model identifies the following variables which must be managed in order to develop into a superior team and achieve superior sustained performance:

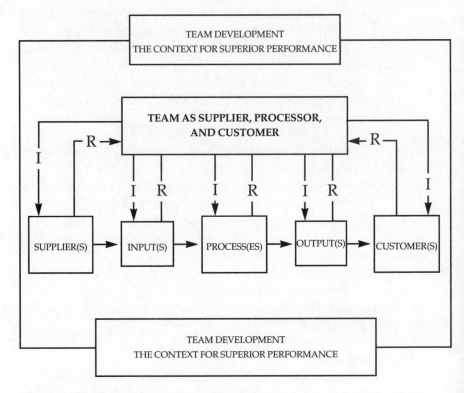

Note: I = Initiating data link; R = Receiving data link

Figure 4.3   General Systems Model of Team Performance

- *Team development: the context of superior performance.* The primary general condition that supports superior performance is superior team development. Development creates the potential for superior performance. In the following chapters the Model for Superior Team Development and Performance will be used to explicate the full meaning of development.
- *Customers.* Teams exist to satisfy their internal and external customers. 'Superior teams,' as a colleague of mine once put it, 'find ways to keep their customers outrageously satisfied.' Customers are any individual or group which uses the services or products of a team.

- *Customer communication link.* This communication link, and all other such links, contain two actions: initiating (I) and receiving (R). The customer communication link consists of the many two-way communication connections that permit the team to: (1) measure how well its customers value what it delivers; (2) anticipate its customers' changing needs and requirements; and (3) discover with its customers how to improve every aspect of its services and products.
- *Output.* Whatever the team delivers to its internal or external customers, including all services and products.
- *Output communication link.* The various ways that the team accesses information about the quality and cost of its services and products and uses this information for continuous improvement.
- *Work processes.* All the sequential and parallel actions that a team takes to produce its output.
- *Input.* The forms, requests, materials, products, services and the like that a team receives and on which it performs one or more operations to turn the input into output.
- *Input communication link.* The various ways that the team accesses information about the quality and cost of the services and products it obtains from its suppliers to use for continuously improving them.
- *Suppliers.* The individuals and groups who provide whatever it is that a team uses to perform its work and produce its output for some internal or external customer.
- *Suppliers' communication link.* The suppliers' communication link consists of the many two-way communication connections that permit the team to: (1) communicate to its suppliers how well it values what suppliers delivers; (2) communicate its changing needs and requirements to its suppliers; and (3) discover with its suppliers how to improve every aspect of its suppliers' services and products.

Critical characteristics
In addition to using the General Systems Model of Team Performance, teams will, of course, want to use the Superior Team Development and Performance Model. As I have already

indicated, one proven way to do this is to use the Superior Team Development Inventory which I designed for this particular purpose. A copy of the Superior Team Development Inventory is to be found in the Appendix, along with instructions for using it.

Team meetings

Team meetings offer yet another opportunity for assessment and improvement. Meetings present an opportunity for unlimited synergistic problem-solving, creativity, learning and improved performance. They also present an opportunity for an enormous waste of time and the mental resources of people. Meetings can occupy a very special place in the economy of team's performance. Meetings, however, can fail to fulfil their potential. Meetings can be the means for team's squandering time and the resources of team members.

Developing and using meeting norms, as I have already suggested, is one way to assess and improve team meetings. Another way is to identify the outcomes that a team must manage in order to have successful meetings. There are at least two kinds of outcomes: (1) products; and (2) process. Desirable product outcomes can be:

- the achieved objectives of meeting
- a solved problem
- a completed project.

Desirable process outcomes can be that:

- communication among members was of high quality
- members did not deviate from the objectives of the meeting
- the resources of all members were fully used
- consensus on all decisions was achieved
- members followed clear, logical sequence in analysing and solving problems.

Step 6: plan and implement team development and improvement projects

Implicit in each of the steps that I have outlined for developing superior teams is the notion of continuous improvement.

Specifying and committing to becoming a superior team carries with it the commitment to improvement. Setting specific performance goals and measuring performance towards these goals also carries with it the idea of improving every aspect of the team's performance. Superior teams do not set goals to just achieve these goals. They set goals to go beyond these goals.

Look at Figure 4.2 again. The process is continuous. Steps one to five lead to Step six: *plan and implement team development and improvement projects*. Since everything in Figure 4.2 defines and reinforces the idea of continuous improvement, it remains now only to describe the characteristics of the projects of continuous improvement. These projects are:

- team centred and team driven
- structured and systematic
- biased towards proactivity
- based on data and measurable
- long term in emphasis.

Team centred and team driven
Improvement projects are team projects. From start to finish, they require the co-operation and collaboration of every team member to be successful. Improvement projects, like every aspect of team performance, must be team centred. This is what gives improvement projects their power and what guarantees their success. Teams improve performance not by improvements being mandated from higher management, but by the consensual will of the team. This does not mean that expectations cannot or should not be set by management. It means that 'management may propose, but teams dispose'. Superior teams continue to exist, not by doing what they did last year or last month, but by *exceeding* what they did last year and last month.

Biased towards proactivity
Continuous improvement means a great deal more than 'putting out fires', or correcting some mistake or attending to some deficit. Such improvements are largely repairs. Superior teams certainly fix things which are broken. Indeed, one of their more obvious

characteristics is that they fix what is broken very quickly and permanently. But they do much more. Superior teams give attention to what is already working well. They analyse just how they are reaching their performance goals in order to find new ways to exceed these goals and to set new goals.

Based on data and measurable

I have already discussed the matter of measuring performance goals. Improvement projects have their own goals. All improvement projects are measurement projects. Improvement projects are not based on bias and whim. They are based on data. Improvement projects define opportunities and problems with numbers and their performance is tracked with numbers.

Improvement projects are based on questions like: How many? How often? How long? To what degree? How much? They start with questions like: How long does the process take? How many pits were there in the part? What is the cost to produce the report? How often do we get a fastener that measures outside the control limits? How much time is spent on correcting design errors?

In this chapter I have set out six steps that teams follow in developing themselves into superior teams. I have discussed in sufficient detail all of the steps except Step 4: select and use Superior Team Development and Performance Model. It is this model, the description of its components and how to use it which are the most distinctive contributions to team formation and development made in this book. The remaining chapters are given over to a discussion of the model.

5 The model for superior team development and performance

The Model for Superior Team Development and Performance, Figure 5.1, underlies everything that is said in this book about the specific task of turning a particular group of people into a superior team. I have taken great pains to ensure that this model is a functional model. It describes what superior teams are like and suggests what leaders and other key participants can do to build them. In this chapter I will sketch out the model, briefly describe its elements and show how these elements are related to each other.

A number of team development and team performance models have been described by other writers (cf. Gouillart and Kelly, 1995; Hackman, 1983; Hensey, 1992; Katzenbach and Smith, 1993; Kolodny and Kiggundu, 1980; Nieva, Fleis and Rieck, 1985; Steiner, 1972; Thambain and Wilemon, 1987). I have referred to these models in conducting my own studies of work teams and have taken them into account in constructing my Model for Superior Team Development and Performance. The Model for Superior Team Development, however, differs in several ways from other models. Important and distinctive characteristics of the model are:

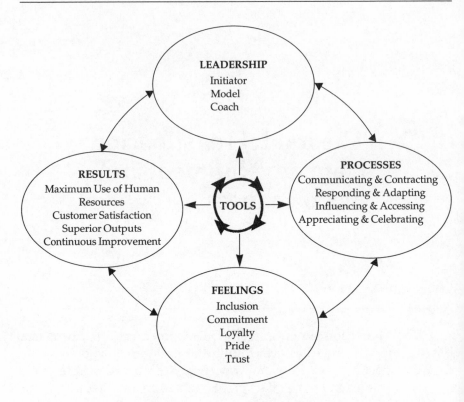

Figure 5.1   Superior Team Development and Performance Model

- The model does not view team development and performance as finally dependent on such variables as the nature of the task and quality of the environment. My model communicates the view that team development and performance are largely a function of a work unit's decision to be a team – regardless of such variables as task and environment.

- The model couples development with performance. The issues for team development and team performance are the same. Team development and team performance occur together. The more highly developed the team becomes, the better the team performance.

- The model is based on a clear distinction between team-building and team development.

- The model emphasizes a set of characteristics that other models do not, for example, informal processes and feelings.
- The model does not just describe teams – it describes *superior* teams.

Characteristics of the model

I have set out to construct a model that:

- would be easily understood
- would be 'lean' and include only information that would produce the most dramatic results
- would show team development and performance as fully integrated activities
- would provide an outline for designing superior team development and ensuring superior performance
- would easily generate team specific strategies for continuous improvement.

Easily understood

The model describes four elements that most people mentioned in my original study and which most people have listed in the years that I and my colleagues have verified the model in our workshops and consulting experiences with organizations. In one way or another, most people describe their best teams with attributes which fall into the following general categories: results, informal processes, feelings and leadership.

The fifth element in the model, tools, is not part of the model proper. This element includes tools that I have developed and used for creating teams with the characteristics of superior teams. The four elements of results, informal processes, feelings and leadership reflect the experiences of the majority of people who have actually been members of real work teams. The model describes exactly what people must take into account if they want superior work teams. The characteristics represent opportunities that must all be addressed, although a team may, from time to time, focus on opportunities represented by one of the characteristics.

Lean

The model includes the bare minimum of what must be taken into account in order to stimulate superior team development and ensure superior performance. There are only four primary elements in the model that describe the characteristics of superior teams. There are doubtless other elements that have some impact on team development and performance, but these four characteristics are so obviously dominant that we know they must always be taken into account in the development of superior teams. We also know that, if teams concentrate on these four characteristics, they will develop themselves into superior teams.

Everything in the model highlights opportunities that every work unit can address. It does not include variables that work teams may not be able to influence, for example, organizational environment or the nature of the tasks to be performed.

Integrating development and performance

The model explicitly declares that team development and team performance are not separable entities. To develop is to perform. To undertake a developmental activity is to take an action that also becomes part of the team's performance and which prepares it for still higher levels of performance. For example, if a team decides to increase the use of team members' competencies, the team is making a decision about its development, but it is also making a decision that will ensure improvement in the quality of its products and services. If a team begins to measure its performance, it will invariably identify opportunities for its further development.

A model to design by

The model clearly targets opportunities for developing teams and improving performance. Within each of the elements, a number of sub-elements or opportunities are listed that help define exactly what work units should do to become superior teams. For example, under Processes, four informal processes are listed: communicating and contacting; responding and adapting; influencing and improving; and appreciating and celebrating. Each of these processes becomes a checkpoint in building a superior team development initiative. All the sub-elements listed under each of the other three elements can be used in a similar way. These sub-elements are the critical leverage points for superior team development.

Identifying specific strategies

The model is a summary of the actual experiences that people undergo when they are engaged in some type of superior team-work or when they are members of superior work teams, and it has been stripped down to contain only the most essential information. Because of these two qualities, the model can easily be translated into very tangible strategies that are relevant to the needs of any team. Take a single example. An engineering design group that was in a seminar of mine decided that it should strengthen the way it showed appreciation to its team members and celebrated individual and team successes. The team was quickly able to describe its current condition. Members had all kinds of examples to illustrate their expectations and they were able to decide exactly what kind of actions they needed to take. The result was they more than doubled the number of formal awards that they obtained for their team and infused far more creative energy into their informal award system.

The model I am describing was derived by studying a great variety of teams and has been applied by a still greater variety of teams as a development tool. The model works to improve the development and performance of critical care units in hospitals, quality assurance groups, accounting units, government offices, multiple staffs of religious organizations, management teams, project teams, production teams and many others. The model applies to any work unit which produces outputs for some internal or external customer and which stays together long enough to assume responsibility for its own team development. There are obviously groups which may meet only once or twice and which are so short-lived that it is inappropriate or impossible for them to undertake any significant team development initiatives.

Model elements

Figure 5.1 displays the Model for Superior Team Development and Performance, identifies the four key characteristics of superior teams and suggests their interactive and interdependent relationships. At the centre of the model are Tools. These are not the typical tools that you find in most books and training manuals on teams, for example, brainstorming, nominal group technique, cause-and-effect diagrams. The tools that I describe are *developmental* tools for building superior teams. I have included in the Appendix three tools which have proven value in developing superior teams: Using the Model for Superior Team Development and Performance; Using the Superior Team Development Inventory; and Using the Systems Team Improvement Model. The four primary characteristics of superior teams are:

1   *Achieving superior team results.* Team results include the final outcomes of: making maximum use of a team's human resources; increasing the number of satisfied customers; delivering outputs of superior services and products (even against all odds); and continuously improving work systems and every aspect of the team's performance.
2   *Informal team processes.* These processes include all the day-to-day activities and actions a team takes to produce results, i.e., the processes of communicating and contacting, responding and adapting, influencing and improving, and appreciating and celebrating. These are not the formal or standard work processes by which products are produced or services are delivered.
3   *Feelings.* Superior teams have members who consistently share certain kinds of feelings which are directly related to the qualities of their team and which influence the qualities of these teams. Among the most important of such feelings are: inclusion, commitment, loyalty, pride and trust.
4   *Leadership.* Superior teams are always characterized by a distinctive kind of team leadership. Such leadership may not be vested in one person, but be shared, as in self-managed teams. As leadership is exercised in superior teams we can

find that certain leadership roles become very obvious. These roles include: initiating team development, modelling the best in teamwork and team membership, and coaching.

Team results

When people talk about the achievements of their superior teams they use phrases like:

- 'We sacrificed personal needs and interests to reach a common goal.'
- 'We were always trying to do things better. Sometimes you felt like every few weeks you were using so many new techniques that you were in a different job.'
- 'What I remember most was the way the people who used our trouble-shooting service felt about us. They thought we walked on water.'
- 'When people finally knocked off we looked like a moving company or a bunch of computer salesmen or something. People took their PCs home at night and did all sorts of new things.'
- 'We all worked very hard, there wasn't much slack, we were on a tight schedule.'
- 'We never gave up, we always found a way to work around obstacles, to solve problems, to fix things.'
- 'We simply did a superior job and outperformed everybody's expectations.'
- 'We could be flexible. We weren't bound by so many rules that we couldn't be inventive.'
- 'There was a lot of excitement. Things were always happening. You could almost feel the energy at times.'

By analysing such comments as these (along with hundreds of others) I have concluded that superior teams consistently accomplish at least the following four outputs (Figure 5.1):

- maximum use of the team's human resources

- highly satisfied customers
- superior output in the face of all odds
- continuous improvement.

Maximum use of the team's human resources

People describe their team's performance as a time in which their competencies (motivation, knowledge, skill and experience) and those of their colleagues were fully utilized – everyone gave 110 per cent. The whole group was energized. People felt driven to succeed.

The people in my studies have talked about 'being stretched'. They talk of 'doing the impossible', of 'pulling off an incredible coup', 'of breakthroughs', of 'feeling bigger than life'. They describe learning new skills and developing new insights. People in superior teams are stimulated to think, to solve problems and to know more about their total organizations than they ever dreamed possible. Members of superior teams have the experience of transcending themselves – of going beyond what they thought were permanent limitations.

Highly satisfied customers

All work units have customers, i.e., other individuals and groups within and without the organization who use their services and products. One mark of poorly performing work units is that they fail to recognize that they have customers or they do not care that they have customers. Such work groups certainly do not make the important distinction between satisfied customers and highly satisfied customers. Superior teams do know they have customers, and they are obsessive about giving their customers each time, and every time, services and products which are 100 per cent fit to use 100 per cent of the time.

Superior teams create superior customers, first, by providing products and services that are fully fit to use. Secondly, they maintain a continuous feedback and follow-up process with their customers. Finally, they work continuously to improve their formal or structured work processes which produce the products and services they deliver to their customers.

The first question that leaders and members of groups should be able to answer is: what practical difference will it make if we become a team? Two answers to this question that we learn from superior teams are:

- Members of the team will make fuller use of the competencies that they now have and they will stay on a steep learning curve to gain new competencies.
- You will become more and more valued because you persist in meeting and exceeding the expectations of your customers.

Another and related answer to the question of what difference it makes to become a team and finally a superior team is that superior teams produce superior results against all odds.

Superior output against all odds

When people talk about their best teams they describe their outputs in terms of exceeding expectation, of going beyond what they and others thought was possible. They talk about being flexible and innovative and of never giving up. In superior teams the adrenalin is flowing, energy levels are high, and members approach their jobs with the expectation that, together, they will find a way to meet the most difficult and unexpected challenges.

Continuous improvement

People often remember their times in superior teams as ones in which they were always reaching a bit higher and challenging the limits. They remember reducing error rates, changing work flow processes, improving customer satisfaction and improving output.

I have described in earlier chapters the many opportunities that teams have to measure and improve every aspect of their performance. For example, Figure 4.3, General Systems Model of Team Performance, and my discussion of the model in Chapter 4 offer a full overview of the many opportunities that teams find to improve their performance. Superior teams continuously work at taking advantage of all these opportunities.

Informal team processes

There are at least four informal processes that superior teams use which are thoroughly ingrained in the way they do business. These processes are not formal systems like purchasing systems or information systems or production systems. These are largely informal processes of interaction. The four informal processes that distinguish superior teams from all other teams are:

- communicating and contacting
- responding and adapting
- influencing and improving
- appreciating and celebrating.

Communicating and contacting

Members of superior work teams talk a great deal, interact a great deal and meet often. They make special efforts to listen to their customers, inside and outside their organizations. What I found in my original study, and what I have verified over and over again, is that superior team members spend time with each other, on and off the job. A sign in one company I visited read, 'Work hard, play hard – and do them together'. Superior teams are always 'seamless' organizations. Job descriptions, protocols and titles are of no final significance. Team goals and team success take precedence over everything else.

Responding and adapting

Members of superior teams respond to each other, to problems, to challenges and to the unexpected, and they often respond in highly creative ways. They are quick to recognize changes as possible opportunities and do not waste much time resisting them as potential catastrophes. Some of the superior teams that I have observed or have had described to me seem to thrive on adversity. They make new discoveries, find new allies and develop clever ways to work around problems.

One team of senior managers that I was assisting in a strategic planning initiative was informed during one of our sessions that corporate headquarters was planning to levy a 10 per cent cut in overhead expenses across the board for all its regional offices. Rather than indulging in an 'ain't-it-awful' routine, i.e. the typical response, this team decided to plan a 20 per cent cut and then work back up to a 10 per cent cut. The logic was that if they could manage really bad news like a 20 per cent cut, then a 10 per cent cut would be child's play.

Influencing and accessing

Superior teams make it easy for people to influence every aspect of the team's work. It follows from this that these teams are always on a positive improvement slope because they access the knowledge, skills and experience of each other. When people join superior teams, they sometimes must make quite an adjustment. One jobholder described it to me this way:

I had been on board for less than a week when we had our first staff meeting. My group was in the process of analysing a particular work flow for handling materials in a metals processing sequence. I knew just enough to feel ignorant. But everyone expected me to join in. In fact the other people made it impossible for me to keep silent. They kept asking me, 'what do you think?' I had more say in that group in the first half hour than I had in the years I had been in my previous job.

In most work units, whether they are teams or not, members have some degree of influence over their jobs. In superior work teams, members have extensive influence over their own work, but they have much more. They have potential influence over every aspect of the whole team's work.

In the traditional work unit, the jobholder is responsible for his or her job and the supervisor is responsible for the unit. In superior work teams all the members can influence all aspects of the team's performance so all members feel responsible for every aspect of the team's performance. In traditional work groups the 'experts' solve problems. In superior work teams everyone solves problems.

Influence is inevitably coupled with continuous improvement. As one manager put it: 'There is nothing more complicated in improving the job than asking the people who do the job how to improve it.' I have verified that manager's statement many times over. I have asked people attending my seminars and workshops to jot down one idea that they firmly believe could improve the quality of their organization's performance. I do not know of a single case in which each person has not written down an idea. People are full of ideas that can improve an organization's performance. One mark of a superior team is that these ideas always receive attention.

Superior teams consistently make the most of their human resources. One reason for this is that they make it easy for people to influence what others know and think, and they make it easy for members to have access to what others know and think.

Appreciating and celebrating

Another process that superior teams use is appreciating and celebrating. Members of superior teams typically describe long hours and, even, stressful hours. They talk about being tired and sometimes exhausted. But they also talk about their experiences as ones in which they were respected and highly thought of. They remember a great deal of kudos and pats on the back.

Members of superior teams do not take each other for granted. When people take on the tough and dirty jobs their peers and their leaders say 'thank you'. And they do it in creative, if not outrageous ways. One of my favourite awards used by one of the teams I studied is called the 'Quiet Excellence Award'. Any team member can nominate another member for the award. It is given to any team member who consistently performs his/her job in an outstanding manner without complaint or fanfare.

Informal processes and results are related and interactive. By communicating and staying in contact with each other, teams are using a process to make maximum use of the team's human resources. By staying in close communication with their customers they are using one important strategy to ensure enthusiastically positive customers. By responding and adapting, superior teams are using a fundamental process for making continuous improvement part of the routine way they do business.

There are two other sets of characteristics of superior teams that are interrelated with results and informal processes. Superior team members share a set of common *feelings* about their work and their team, and superior teams develop a characteristic style of *leadership*.

Team feelings

People who have described their experiences on superior teams usually include implicit and explicit information about the way they felt as members of their teams. The kinds of remarks they make are:

- 'Nobody was left out, we all felt that we were in this together.'
- 'We respected each other, we took each other's ideas seriously, nobody got put down.'
- 'You felt you could count on the other people. If they said they were going to do something, they did it.'
- 'Sometimes it felt like a family. We were really close.'
- 'People didn't hide anything. We kept everything above board. If something wasn't right and people were not getting along, we fixed it.'
- 'People didn't try to embarrass each other. It was like people would go out of their way to make somebody else look good.'
- 'We were like a juggernaut. Nobody was going to get in our way.'
- 'Sometimes you had to stop and remind yourself that you had a family and other things to take care of besides the job. It just felt so important to get the job done that you sometimes forgot about everything else.'
- 'It was easy to get confused about who had what job. We all jumped in to take care of whatever needed doing.'
- 'You never had to ask for help. If someone had a little slack they would start working with the person who was snowed under.'

From these and the hundreds of other statements that I have recorded, I have identified five feelings that people describe so often that there is little doubt that they are characteristic of the best teams on which people have served. These feelings are: (1) inclusion; (2) commitment; (3) loyalty; (4) pride; and (5) trust.

Inclusion

The managers and employees who have described their experiences in superior teams consistently use phrases like 'there was a sense of togetherness', 'no one felt left out', 'everyone shared in the tough times and the good times', 'there was a real joy of being in the thing together', and 'we had a real sense of camaraderie'. One dominant characteristic of a superior team is that its members feel included. They feel included in the planning and problem-solving processes that affect them, they have access to the information they need, and they feel included in the work and purposes of the whole group.

Commitment

A second feeling that team members report is a strong sense of commitment to the team's goal and the team's success. The way that this commitment is often described is in the way team members record sacrificing their personal needs. As the manager of a subsystem in NASA's Viking Project put it: 'For the duration of the project, I told my family that we were in this together. There was no way that our lives would go on as usual. Until launch, the project would be our first commitment.'

Loyalty

A third feeling that characterizes the experience of people on superior teams is loyalty to the team and to each other. In a rocket flow processing group a technician told this story:

Charlie was very sick. We didn't know when he would get back. We had a tough choice to make. Our group leader offered to get us a replacement. But we just couldn't do that to Charlie. We said we would catch up the slack until Charlie was back on his feet. And we did, but it cost each of us some Saturdays and Sundays to do it.

A senior executive described his best team experience with these words:

What I really remember about my directorate was that you never took cheap shots at anybody. And if you even tried to complain to a third party about another person or work group, you knew very quickly that the third party wasn't interested.

Pride

A fourth feeling that members of superior teams have is pride. When I have explored with managers and employees what they mean by pride, they associated their feelings with being success-ful against all kinds of obstacles and with doing something that was really meaningful. People do not believe that you can have good teams for long that consistently lose.

Time and time again, during my interviews and seminars, managers and employees have contrasted their good teams with their bad ones. They remembered bad experiences as those in which their teams failed to meet milestones, had large budget overruns, and took on projects that were later abandoned.

Trust

A fifth feeling that people on superior teams experience is trust. 'When one of us said we would do something, you never had to ask again or follow up. You just knew it would be done,' was the way a systems analyst put it. A member of a logistics support group said about his team members: 'We were all professionals. Every one of us was as good as you could get. If we didn't have the answers, there weren't any to be had.'

It is not possible from my studies to tell which comes first, feel-ings, informal processes or results, e.g., whether a superior team makes full use of its human resources and achieves superior per-formance which then results in certain feelings in team members, or vice versa. What is clear, however, is that superior teams pro-duce superior results, employ distinctive informal processes and their members share a set of special feelings. It is also clear that all of these characteristics are in continuous interaction with each other.

In addition to results, processes and feelings superior teams have a fourth distinguishing characteristic. They develop a special kind of leadership.

Developing a special kind of leadership

Leadership in superior teams is qualitatively different from leadership in other work units. Leadership in superior teams has special characteristics, whether there is a formal leader or whether leadership is shared by team members.

Leading in superior work teams is not primarily a use of power and influence to develop followers who respond in some direction that has been directed by others. Leadership in superior teams has a radically different orientation than that of traditional leadership. Leadership in superior teams is accomplished as a team function. It is accomplished with and through the team. It is accomplished by women and men who are first, last and always team players and team members. One member of an industrial shop described his team leader this way:

This guy was a team player all the way. He never played God and acted like he always knew best about everything. If we had a special project coming down he always called us together to map out how we would take on the job. If anybody had an idea about how to make something better, he was always prepared to listen. And when we were doing some particularly dirty job he was usually there pitching in and doing his bit.

Leadership in superior teams has two special meanings. It means:

- leading through teamwork
- keeping in mind both the team's potential to perform (i.e., its development) and ensuring that the team meets or exceeds all of its performance goals.

Leading through teamwork

Team leaders are team members and team players. They lead through teamwork. They view all work as an opportunity for teamwork. The practical meaning of this orientation is that team leadership is always focused:

- on team performance more than individual performance
- on commitment as the way to achieve superior performance and not control.

Keeping in mind both the team's development and its performance

Superior team leaders also have a second special orientation. They view team development and team performance as inseparable. They know that the more fully developed the team becomes the greater its potential to excel in every other aspect of its performance.

Superior leadership, whether shared by the team or exercised by an individual, gives attention (cognitively or intuitively) to the basic steps in team development described in Chapter 4. They help the team:

1 Make and remake the decision to become a superior team.
2 Set, enforce, and revise team norms.
3 Set team performance goals and measures.
4 Use the Model for Superior Team Development and Performance as a guide.
5 Assess and evaluate current levels of team development and performance.
6 Plan and implement team development and performance improvement projects.

Superior leadership functions

There are at least three functions which I have been able to associate clearly with the leadership in superior work teams. These functions are:

- initiator
- model
- coach.

Initiator

Leadership is exercised in superior teams by appointed leaders or members initiating the various actions and processes for building their work units into superior teams. Leadership is expressed by anyone who sees an opportunity to improve the way the team conducts its business. At one time this may mean helping the team clarify its performance goals. At another time it may mean testing the team's will to become a superior team. At yet another time it will mean testing and modifying team norms. The point to be emphasized is that leadership exists by taking action to ensure that the team's potential to perform is always being improved.

Model

Superior team leaders model the kind of performance and behaviour that help develop their team. Superior team leaders are first of all superior team members. Leadership is modelled on superior teams in two ways. First, leaders model teamwork in the way they conduct their own business and perform their own tasks. Second, they model team membership in the way they interact with their fellow team members.

Coach

Coaching includes a multitude of informal conversations that people on teams have with other team members. In these conversations they carry out such functions as:

- *solving problems* that others present them
- *tutoring* and helping team members develop new competencies
- *challenging* team members to improve their performance and take on more challenging tasks
- *giving feedback* to each other to ensure that everyone is on track.

Leadership is the third element in the Model for Superior Team Development and Performance. I turn now to discuss briefly the fifth and final element in the model, tools.

Tools for developing superior teams

At the centre of the Model for Superior Team Development and Performance are the tools by which a team can undertake the practical business of becoming a superior team. These tools are by no means a fixed set. I have, however, already mentioned three such tools, and I will treat these fully in the Appendix.

The criteria that I have used in selecting the tools that I have included in the Appendix have certain characteristics. First, each tool is one that I have used in hundreds of workshops and team development projects. Each of the tools has proven merit. Second, I have selected tools that can *only* be used by teams. These tools force teamwork. They have little or no value if used by individuals in some sort of unilateral action to improve their teams. Third, I have selected only tools that have a clear conceptual basis for action. Each tool is in fact a descriptive model that has various elements which are clearly related. Fourth, these tools include only those which will have multiple impacts on team development and performance, i.e., each tool will tend to strengthen a team's results, informal processes, feelings and leadership, while at the same time improving the other aspects of its work.

In this chapter I have introduced the Model for Superior Team Development and Performance. In the following chapters I will describe in detail each of the four elements in the model which distinguish superior teams from all other groups and teams.

6 Focusing on results

For organizations, the main pay-off from superior work teams is that these teams consistently produce superior results. The only reason for organizations to develop superior work teams is the same reason for which they acquire new technology, downsize, restructure, modify work sequences or introduce management information systems. The reason is (or at least it should be) to achieve results which ensure their long-term success. Achieving superior results is the first and most important characteristic of superior teams. The results that superior teams consistently achieve are:

- maximum use of the team's human resources
- highly satisfied customers
- superior performance in the face of all odds
- continuous improvement.

One theme that I have been presenting throughout this book is that team development and team performance are not separate entities. The kind of performance that is required today, i.e., sustained superior performance, can only come from highly developed teams. Teamwork is the integrating activity in work units and organizations that leverages small improvements into very large ones. We can only expect to achieve a competitive advantage if we make full use of the integrating and transforming power that is potentially resident in teams.

It is clearly the case that teams become superior teams because they want to produce superior results and believe that they can produce such results. When teams determine that they will create enthusiastically positive customers, they have *explicitly* targeted a superior outcome, but they have also *implicitly* launched a process to development themselves into the kinds of teams that can achieve such results.

In the last chapter, I presented a brief overview of the four main characteristics of superior teams. One of these characteristics is superior results. In this chapter I will provide a full description of the four superior results that superior teams produce.

Maximum use of team's human resources

The Springfield Re-manufacturing Company, SRC, was featured a few years ago on a USA news programme. Jack Stack, the President of SRC, reported a remarkable turn-round in this company that overhauls old truck engines. So remarkable was the turn-round that Mercedes began sending its engines *from Germany* to SRC for overhaul rather than having them done in Germany. Sales for the company tripled in six years.

Not only did SRC develop all of its work units into superior teams, it turned the whole organization into a superior team. The president of the company contributes the company's turn-round to a programme called, 'The Game of Business'. The game has three rules:

1   Know the rules.
2   Learn to read the score.
3   Hold a stake in the game.

These rules provided SRC with a structure for making full

use of the human resources of its teams. Here are a few examples.

Under rule one, everyone was expected to know everyone else's job in the work team. Because each team member had this greater competency, the typical cycle of too much work and too little work was eliminated. When one team member had a period of slack in his/her job, that team member immediately started working with a fellow team member who had a backlog.

Under rule two, every person was taught how to read the company's financial reports and to know what implications the numbers had for profit and loss. Every person in SRC knew how the company made money, if the company was making money, and exactly how his/her job influenced the outcomes.

Under rule three, the employees and managers own the company. All decisions that affect the company are made by employees and managers.

A few years ago the company was faced with the choice of either paying out a bonus or using the extra cash to liquidate the company's debt, thus making the stock more valuable. The employees voted not to take the bonus.

Superior teams make the most of their people. Members are always on a learning curve. They do not just learn a job, they learn the team's whole business. None of their work processes 'hiccup' because a key member happens to be absent. Their jobs are what they do, but the team is what they own. Members feel fully responsible for everything that happens in their team. As one rate clerk put it:

You were expected to know your job and the rest of the jobs in the office as well. About the worst thing that you could do was to tell a customer to call back because there was no one in the office who could answer a question or compute the correct shipping rate.

Making the most of a team's resources means at least the following:

1   Expecting people to be competent.

2   Giving people the opportunity to show that they are competent.
3   Giving people the support required to become more competent.

I am using competent to include the knowledge, skill and experience that people must have to do a job. I am also including in competent the idea of confidence. People are not fully competent until they have the confidence to use the knowledge, skill and experience that they possess.

Expecting people to be competent

For some 30 years I served as one of the primary consultants to the USA's National Aeronautics and Space Administration (NASA), doing most of my work for Headquarters and the John F. Kennedy Space Center. During this time, I also worked with many of NASA's contractors. In all of my direct contacts with hundreds of leaders and teams, I do not ever recall hearing anyone complain that a fellow team member was technically incompetent. I heard many complaints about 'overdirecting', 'micromanaging', 'lack of co-operation', 'the inability to work with others', and 'lack of teamwork'. The only suggestion that I ever heard about someone being 'incompetent' was directed at supervisors and managers. Upon analysis, what this criticism meant was these leaders had poor communication skills, did not listen very well and failed to make the best use of their employees' competencies.

People can be competent because they want to be viewed as competent and to think of themselves as competent. It is simply not the case that people anywhere, in any significant numbers, set out to be incompetent and demonstrate how well they can fail. The greatest impairment to developing the competency of people is the expectations that we have of what they can do.

Traditional leadership has too often focused on the failures of people, rather than the failures of the tools and work systems that people use and the environment in which they work. When people do not have access to the information they need, when they do not have easy access to the help they need, when they are punished for trying, when they are asked to spend time on non-productive activities, when they do not have the freedom to act and when they are not involved in solving their own work problems, they will appear incompetent. What they are, of course, are victims of bad management.

The biggest obstacle for organizations to overcome in the process of becoming team centred and developing superior work teams are the expectations of organizational leaders about the competency of their employees. Superior team members become self-managing and self-controlling. In the several companies where I have worked to establish self-managed teams, it has been the indecision and ambivalence of the companies' leaders about the ability of their employees to manage their teams that has always been a large obstacle. It is not what these leaders say, it is what they do.

I remember watching a software design team take a sharp downward turn in its performance after it changed team leaders. The first leader involved all members in the design of each new project, assigned each new team member a mentor and held regular seminars led by team members on some aspect of their work or on some new technology development. The new team leader, fancying himself an authority on all aspects of the team's work, stopped involving all members in project design and eliminated most of the other strategies used by his predecessor to maximize team members' competencies. One clear indicator of the new leader's impact was that (within a year) most team members transferred out of the unit and the remainder were in the process of doing so. The condition of this team was worse after opportunities to be competent were shut off than it was before these opportunities had been started.

A short time ago I helped a government agency in the USA begin to experiment with self-managed teams. There are several steps in building a self-managed team. An important first step is that the people on the team should be physically located together. Another early step is that the team must develop its own internal structure and work processes. In this agency the senior executive responsible for developing these experimental teams provided no assistance to relocate the team members to the same area, and shortly after the teams were organized he demanded regular reports on the services and products the teams were producing. Without time to develop and without team members working in proximity to each other, the outputs of the teams were (predictably) poor. The senior executive concluded that the employees involved in the experiment could not manage themselves.

Giving people the opportunity to show that they are competent

An outcome from one of my seminars on team-centred continuous improvement was that a mechanical engineering design team greatly expanded the use of the competencies of its drafters. The situation prior to making changes in the way the drafters worked was:

- Engineers dictated work assignments. The workload fluctuated from too much and large backlogs to too little and the drafters sitting around waiting for their next assignments.
- The drafters did only drafting. They had a very limited opportunity to learn new knowledge and skills. The result was boredom and low morale.
- There were periods of a large backlog because only the engineers could set priorities. They could take the drafters off one job and put them on another. The drafters were forced to be less productive than they might have been because they lost so much time stopping one job, gearing up for a new job, stopping that job and gearing up for another job.

The current status of affairs is that now:

- Drafters and engineers review a project together from the moment of inception.
- Drafters now research the system documentation required

before each new project. They collect the floor plans from facility books, get the appropriate system drawings, etc.

- Drafters do field research along with the engineers and collaborate with the engineers in visualizing the total requirements of the new project.
- Drafters perform the technical assessment of new projects with the engineers and develop cost estimates.
- Drafters perform verification of as-built conditions, i.e., verify that the project was built to specifications and close out the required documentation.

The quantity and quality of the output of this team has greatly improved since it began to make better use of the resource that its drafters represented. This improvement has been acknowledged by the company. During a recent year, the team received six team awards for its performance.

Because of the great success that this mechanical engineering design team had in making a fuller use of its drafters, the company is now using drafters to do all the work on small designs, from conceptualization, to researching the documentation, to drawing the design, to as-built verification. The drafters had always been competent to perform the additional tasks that they are now performing. All they needed was the chance. Now they do more, and the engineers are free to do more. Everybody wins.

People are naturally disposed to demonstrate their competencies. Given half a chance, people will use more and more of their competencies to achieve the goals of their teams. Because people have such a strong drive to demonstrate what they know and what they can do, all that is typically required to get people to demonstrate their competencies in a team is to give them the chance. We have examples on every hand of workers going out of their way to apply their competencies, even fighting management and overcoming other barriers to do so.

Giving people the support required to become more competent

Competency is, first of all, a function of learning. Team members must certainly develop enough confidence to demonstrate the use of their knowledge or skill but, first, they must have the knowledge or skill. Support in a team to ensure that team members become more competent comes down, then, to two factors: (1) learning something; and (2) having a safe place to learn.

Learning on teams

Superior teams are always exciting learning communities. There is never an instance in which each member cannot be sometimes a learner and sometimes a teacher.

One of the most common statements provided by people when they think of their best teams is that 'it was a place to learn'. When I have asked people in my seminars and workshops to tell me why their teams were such a good place to learn, I get responses that fall into the following groups:

- On teams, members are in constant contact in order to achieve the team's goals. They are always asking questions and giving answers that stimulate and provide new insights.
- Teams are usually composed of people from different cultural backgrounds. Often cultural diversity is designed into teams. To make the team work members must learn about each other's cultural norms.
- Teams are always solving problems. Each member will typically learn a variety of approaches and tools for problem-solving, just by the experience of working with their colleagues to solve problems.
- Synergetic learning exists in teams. Mutual stimulation, challenging, and testing create ideas beyond what any one person could produce.
- There is always a mix of competencies on any team. A superior team is a place where these competencies are recognized and used to develop further the competencies of all team members.

- Teams are places where everyone must learn a set of new team skills, e.g., skills for interacting, managing meetings and developing the team.

A safe place to learn

Superior teams provide the best place to learn. Every member of a superior team knows that he/she depends on the competent performance of every other member. Team success depends on the contributions of every member. No member wants another member to fail.

It is not an uncommon experience in the workplace for employees to use knowledge as an instrument of power over other employees. Knowledge can become a way of competing against other employees. In superior teams, members do not compete against each other. Individuals can only succeed as the team succeeds. One of the ways that superior teams ensure the competency of their colleagues is through coaching.

A very successful computer systems consulting firm makes it a policy that each new member of a project team is assigned a coach who is an expert in the technical area in which the new member will work. A marketing team in a large communications company asks each member to take turns conducting a team coaching session in subjects that affect the present and future performance of the team.

Special competencies for being team members

It is characteristic of superior teams that they make the maximum use of their human resources. In the previous sections I have described why teams provide such great potential for developing and using the competencies of their members. What I have been emphasizing is that people can be more competent in a team environment than they can be on their own, and a team's total competency can greatly exceed the collective competency of its members. In superior teams people are in touch and interact freely. People share their competencies with each other. Ideas from one person are built on and improved by other members. Insights from one member stimulate new insights from another person. Members teach other members.

These highly dynamic processes of sharing information, learning from each other, challenging each other and teaching each other, create a special environment for making the very best use of a team's human resources. For teams to create such an environment the team members need to develop the following kinds of competencies:

- rational problem-solving skills
- interpersonal problem-solving skills
- team meeting effectiveness skills.

Rational problem-solving skills

These skills help team members conduct efficient and effective problem-solving discussions and meetings by building structures for developing information, analysing information, identifying alternative strategies and making decisions. The way these structures affect competencies is to:

- increase the use made of individual team member competencies
- add new competencies through increased synergism.

Structured problem-solving environments increase the possibility that all the human resources in a team will be used. In unstructured environments input is often determined by the relative position and authority that people have or the personal relationships that exist on the team or just how aggressive or self-confident a team member might be. Structure can create clarity about direction and process. The result is to increase the comfort level of team members and to free them to participate more actively.

Structured problem-solving also increases team competency because structure makes it easier for team members to build on what others contribute and structure keeps developing ideas from being lost. When teams interact in a random and unstructured way a lot of information and new ideas can just 'fall through the cracks' and go uncaptured and unremembered.

Structured problem-solving also makes it easier for team members to develop new competencies. Problem-solving structures can be thought to give order to the synergistic quality of a team's interactions. Synergism describes a process in which ideas trigger new ideas, insights trigger new insights and opportunities trigger new opportunities. Synergism is the increase in total knowledge, skill and wisdom that can take place through the interaction of team members. The new knowledge, skill and insight produced through synergism becomes the property of all the team members. Outcomes produced through synergism typically mean that everyone has learned something new.

Interpersonal problem-solving skills

A second set of necessary special team competencies is interpersonal problem-solving skills. These are the skills that underlie the ability of team members to interact in ways that maximize their ability to perform all their team development and team performance tasks while maintaining positive relationships with each other. I have discussed at some length the process and skills associated with successful interpersonal problem-solving communication in an earlier book (Kinlaw, 1989).

To make the most of a team's potential, members must have the interpersonal competency to create conversations with each other which have two key characteristics: respect and mutuality (Kinlaw, 1989, 1990).

Respect
Respect is a function of the amount of information that is developed between team members, and it is a function of the ease with which information is developed between members. Team members feel respected when other team members listen to them, encourage them to give information and to offer ideas. They do not feel respected when their ideas are rejected without a fair hearing, when they are ridiculed or when they are patronized.

Mutuality

Mutuality carries the meaning of reciprocal or balanced. In the most successful conversations, team members involve each other fully in the communication process. The best problem-solving conversations consist of mutual exploration and discovery. These conversations are built on team members' recognition that each person brings something special to each conversation. One team member knows some things and the other members know some different things. One member will look at a problem from one perspective and others will have different perspectives. Good problem-solving conversations make the most out of the diversity that team members represent.

Team members need special team skills in order for teams to make the most of the resource that team members represent. The first two kinds of skills that I have discussed are: rational problem-solving skills and interpersonal problem-solving skills. There is a third set of skills that concerns team members' ability to function as value-added participants in team meetings.

Team meeting effectiveness skills

Team meetings are integral to the development of teams into superior teams. Team meetings are required for the continuing processes of sharing information and ideas, of setting goals, of making decisions, of solving problems, and of introducing and managing change. We can expect more and more that jobholders will be members of several teams at the same time. They will be members of their own permanent work team, but they will likely serve as members of a variety of temporary teams and special focus teams like productivity teams, interface teams, tiger teams, action teams and the like. Team members need the skills to organize team meetings and the skills to function as team members and leaders during team meetings.

I will not give here a detailed description of the various skills that are necessary to make team meetings effective and efficient. A number of useful books have already been published on this subject (Borman and Borman, 1972; Bradford, 1976; Kinlaw, 1993, 1996).

The first result identified in the Model for Superior Team

Development and Performance that superior teams achieve is the maximum use of the team's human resources. In the next section I will discuss the second result that superior teams character- istically achieve, highly satisfied customers.

Highly satisfied customers

Total customer satisfaction is always a team effort. Even before companies began to understand that teams were the primary units of performance, and not individuals, no one person in an organization was ever able to satisfy an internal or external cus- tomer without a great deal of co-operation and support from many other individuals and groups within the organization. Figure 6.1 highlights the many differences that exist between an individual focus on customer service and a team-centred focus.

Superior teams create highly satisfied customers for a number of reasons. Figure 6.1 summarizes the following points:

1   Every team customer is my customer and each of my cus- tomers is a team customer. The situation then cannot exist that a customer is not treated as a customer and responded to as a customer, regardless of whom the customer has worked with in the past. No customer is ever put 'on hold' or referred to some other person or resource. Whoever happens to be in touch with a team's customer assumes full responsibility for the satisfaction of that customer.
2   Teams bring all of their resources to bear on satisfying a cus- tomer. Members are in easy contact with all other members to help solve any customer question and respond to any cus- tomer need.
3   Teams respond continuously to the needs of customers. Responding to a customer never depends on the presence of a particular team member. The *team* satisfies customers. *Individual* team members, working independently, cannot satisfy customers. Whether a particular team member is pre- sent or available or not does not determine how well the cus- tomer's needs are managed. Customers do not care if a

TEAM-CENTRED		INDIVIDUAL
	Whose customer?	
Team's		Mine
	Response	
Total		Piecemeal
Continuous		Intermittent
	Success criteria	
Team performance		Personal performance
	Relationships	
Co-operative		Competitive
Interdependent		Dependent
	Rewards	
Team		Individual
	Improvements	
Integrated resources		Fragmented resources
Fast		Slow
Continuous		Sporadic
Proactive		Reactive

Figure 6.1   Team-centred customer service

particular person is sick or on holiday. Customers want a response and teams are the only way to ensure a response. Teams do not depend on the presence of any one team member to respond.

4 Teams respond best to customers because teams measure their performance by their total team performance, and not the performance of individual team members. If any customer is not managed successfully, it is never the problem of one team member, it is the problem of the team.

5 Teams are able to provide continuous support and response to customers. Individuals are only able to respond when they are personally available.

6 Individuals on superior teams do not compete with each other to satisfy their own individual customers. Members exist in a co-operative and interdependent relationship to serve the needs of all the team's customers.

7 Teams are rewarded for satisfying the needs of the team's customers, not for individuals satisfying the needs of their own customers.

8 Teams are able to respond to the needs of their customers in ways that are quite beyond the resources of individuals. Teams have resources that far exceed those of individuals. Because teams have multiple and backup resources and competencies, they are able to respond quickly to the needs of their customers. Because a team response to the needs of customers does not depend on the presence or competence of any one individual, teams can provide continuous service to customers that is not interrupted by the presence or availability of any one member.

9 Finally, teams (especially superior teams) do not wait for customers to communicate a need. On the basis of the synergetic relationship that exists among team members, they are proactive in discovering the expectations of customers.

Teams satisfy customers at levels that are quite beyond the power of individuals. Superior teams satisfy customers at levels that are quite beyond the power of ordinary teams.

Superior output against all odds

Superior teams deliver superior results often in the face of un-
believably difficult conditions. An Air Force technician in a mis-
sile group described this averted catastrophe:

We had a false alert and the missiles were automatically armed
with nuclear warheads. The silos were open. How we ever got all
the co-operation that we needed in the time we had, I'll never
know. It was just one of those things. We knew we had to do it. It
was impossible to think of failure and the consequences.

A test conductor for an aerospace manufacturing group remembered the following experience on his superior test team:

We were told at the time that there was no overtime left. We were
at the limits that the company had established. But we all knew
that we had to make the schedule. Not to make the schedule was
unthinkable. So we just shut the doors, and everyone worked for
free. And it was like no one even had to say that was what we were
going to do. Somebody just shut the doors and we kept working.

A supervisor in a project group talked about his team's refusal to
accept any problem as unsolvable: 'We had a word for getting
things done in spite of every possible screw up. The word was
"workarounds". At every status review, if anyone had a problem
nobody left the table until we had figured out a satisfactory
"workaround"'.

None of the people who have given me information about
their best teams has ever suggested that these teams were able to
do 'satisfactory work' because they had all the time, money and
people they needed. Most people mentioned some set of circumstances that made their achievement particularly difficult.

The best teams that people seem to remember most readily are
teams that did something special, i.e., performed in a particularly
outstanding way. But what is more striking than this superior
performance or achievement is that it was gained over, through
and around all sorts of obstacles and unexpected events. The

best teams often push their resources and their people to the limits.

Based on the way that people describe their superior teams, I have come to accept two things about these teams and the obstacles they overcome. First, superior teams have a way of just naturally creating obstacles. They tend to commit themselves to goals that often border on being impossible. Second, they sometimes become so intense and focused in going after their 'impossible' goals that they may encounter a good bit of resistance from people who cannot change and who do not know how to get out of the way.

There is apparently an interactive effect between being a superior team and achieving a superior result. It is impossible to know which happens first or which causes the other. What I do know is that achieving superior output is always a hallmark of superior teamwork and superior teams.

I suppose that the foregoing paragraph can be viewed as simplistic, self-evident, redundant or tautological. I seem to be defining a *superior* team as a *superior* team. But this is not quite so obvious or simple as it might seem.

I have asked hundreds of people to talk to me about their best teams. They could have talked about teams in which everyone was friendly or ones in which they enjoyed themselves or ones in which there was a relaxed atmosphere. Of course, a few people did talk in this way but they were, indeed, very few. The most typical responses to the open-ended question, 'Tell me about your best work team', are the kinds of statements that I have included throughout this book. It has been a rare experience for me that people, when given the chance to talk about their best teams, have not talked about some very special kinds of achievement.

There are several important insights that can be drawn from this connection of superior performance and superior teams which can be used to evolve and select strategies for challenging teams to new levels of superior performance.

Clear, meaningful goals and values that team members influence

A consistent finding of myself and other researchers is that work teams that are clear about their goals and values (which they perceive as meaningful) will consistently outperform teams that do not have such clarity (Ellis and Tonkin, 1995; Kinlaw, 1989, 1995; Locke *et al.*, 1981; Varney, 1989). We can perceive a hierarchy in the impact that goals and values have on output. Clarity alone about goals and values will have a positive impact on performance. When goals and values are, in addition to being clear, perceived as being meaningful, they will have an even stronger impact on output. The full impact of goals and values is realized when team members influence what these goals and values are.

When team members are involved in setting team goals and values they are, of course, helping to ensure that these goals and values are clear and meaningful to them. But influence creates the sense of ownership which, in turn, helps to generate the sense of commitment that is essential to sustained superior output.

A second factor that has great potential to move a team towards sustained superior output is the degree to which a team has clear goals and values created by the team itself. A third factor is the tendency of teams (when given the chance) to set very high goals for themselves.

Teams will set higher output goals when they themselves set the goals

A few years ago I consulted with a wind tunnel test team to establish output measures. My first step was to get the team to identify its key results, to set measures to track these results and to accept responsibility for these results. One key result that the team identified was technical papers. When I started working with the team, it averaged eight papers a year. After the team became involved in measuring its results, it voluntarily set a goal to double its old output. It established a goal of 20 technical reports per year.

Some time ago members of a printing branch attended a total quality management seminar of mine. During the seminar these team members decided to review the goals that management had set for them for production and quality. One of the several goals that the team set for itself was to halve the error rate currently targeted for them by management. Within six months they achieved this goal which they had voluntarily set and which greatly exceeded anything management felt possible. When work teams began to set production goals at a General Electric plant they set their goals 50 per cent higher than management expected.

The second result that superior teams typically achieve is superior output against all odds. Concentrating on output is a significant vehicle for developing superior teams. In selecting strategies to improve output the following considerations should be kept in mind:

- Superior output against all odds can only be achieved when people are fully committed to the team's goals and values.
- People become fully committed to a team's goals and values when these goals and values are clear, have meaning and reflect something over which they had some influence.
- A team, when given a chance, will set higher output goals for itself than those set by some external authority.

The fourth output identified in the Model for Superior Team Development and Performance is Continuous Improvement.

Continuous improvement

Continuous improvement is a difficult idea for jobholders to understand. My experience in presenting the idea to managers and employees in various seminars and team development programmes over the years is that most participants respond to the idea of continuous improvement with a good bit of hostility. There are a number of reasons for this.

First, continuous improvement is not an expectation that is built into the culture of most organizations. You will not find continuous improvement in job descriptions and you will not find continuous improvement as a priority among managers. It is not that people are against continuous improvement, it is just that they have difficulty becoming true zealots for improvement because their businesses and unions have been so successful in conditioning them:

- to do their jobs the way the jobs were set up when they took their jobs
- to believe that improvement is not their business, but the business of management or somebody 'up there'
- to believe that they are already doing about all they can do and do not have time to worry about improvements
- to have little commitment to improvement because they do not believe they will realize any real benefit from it
- to resist any change as disruptive, including improvement.

In addition to these conditioning factors there are other reasons that keep work units from committing themselves to continuous improvement. First, continuous improvement is not a clear, unambiguous organizational value that is fully supported and fully rewarded and, second, people often do not have the tools for continuous improvement.

Continuous improvement takes time. For teams to improve everything they do, they must have time to identify improvement opportunities and time to take action and test alternatives. It is difficult for teams to develop themselves into superior teams and to improve their total performance if they have not received some sort of permission. That permission is a cornerstone to the success of high-performing teams.

The key to continuous improvement is teamwork and team development. Teams create possibilities for improvement that are simply not possible in work units that are managed by control and which depend largely on individual effort.

Opportunities for improvement are everywhere. One clear opportunity is in the area of rework and repair. Experts in continuous improvement estimate that a third of what we do consists of redoing what was done before. But opportunities also exist in every work process, in every supply action, in response times and in every repair cycle. Opportunities exist in every aspect of a team's development and performance.

Teams are synonymous with improvement. It is through teams that most of the important improvements in the performance of organizations is taking place. There can now be no question that teams are the main source of improvements like:

- improved quality in service and products
- reduction of absenteeism and turnovers
- cost reductions in materials and personnel
- the commitment to continuous improvement.

During a period when I was actively delivering total quality seminars for NASA, we often used a follow-up process to help us track just what results the seminar achieved. Here are a few of the improvements achieved by a sample of the 300 teams which attended the seminar:

- computerized project-tracking reports that have increased accuracy and reduced time in monitoring projects and reporting their status
- 50 per cent reduction of space required for storage of materials
- significant reduction of unsafe tools
- cross-training in many different groups such as a systems configuration management team, a procurement office, a design engineering branch, a security control group and the like
- team management of overtime roster and shift schedule
- use of work flow diagrams to teach new team members their jobs
- development of baseline performance data by team surveys
- regularized update and feedback sessions with customers.

The fourth largest investor-owned electric utility in the USA, Florida Power and Light (FPL) has more than 3 million customers and 18 000 employees. I noted earlier in this book that FPL was the first recipient of the Deming Prize in the USA. Florida Power and Light is organized into 1 700 quality teams. The Deming Prize citation for FPL noted such improvements as:

- reduction of lost-time injuries from more than one per hundred employees to 0.42 per hundred
- reduction of customer complaints to its lowest level in ten years
- reduction of customer service interruptions from 100 minutes to 48 minutes.

It is inconceivable that these improvements at FPL could have occurred through any other means than teamwork. There is no other known way of harnessing the human and technical potential of an organization for such a level of sustained improvement in performance.

In this chapter I have described in detail what results superior teams consistently achieve. Results are the first characteristic of superior teams. In the next chapter I will describe the next characteristic of superior teams, the kinds of informal processes that they create for undertaking their day-to-day work.

7 Focusing on informal processes

The four characteristics of superior teams included in the Model for Superior Team Development and Performance are: results, informal processes, feelings and leadership. In the previous chapter, I discussed results and its four sub-elements:

- making maximum use of the team's human resources
- creating highly satisfied customers
- producing superior outputs (services and products) against all odds
- continually improving the team's total performance.

In this chapter, I will describe in detail the informal processes.

Superior teams (and work units that periodically rise to the level of superior teamwork) typically develop and use at least four characteristic informal processes. As we saw in Chapter 5, these processes are:

- communicating and contacting
- responding and adapting

- influencing and improving
- appreciating and celebrating.

A consistent finding from our research into superior teams is that members from superior teams describe their teams as places of fluid interaction and easy conversation. They talk about the many different informal acts and behaviours of team members that turn their teams into ones that pulsed with life and energy. A member of a launch test team described her experience:

I felt really 'up' at work. In fact, I felt excited just thinking about what we were doing and the people I was working with. One of the things I remember the clearest was that everybody's job was everybody's job. We all looked to each other to get the whole job done. I don't remember anyone every saying they were too busy to help me and I don't remember ever being surprised about some change or the impact of some delay or things like that. Most of all I remember feeling that no one was going to leave me alone with my problems. Come to think of it, we never thought much about who had what problem, just how to fix the damn thing.

There is a division in a large US company with which I consulted for many years that has a number of the characteristics that I associate with superior teams. I have heard the manager of that division speak on several occasions about his own organizational philosophy. The way he describes his division is:

I consider organizational charts and job descriptions to be what we use to explain to outsiders who we are and what we do. But there isn't much about those diagrams that describes how we actually work together. My experience is that we have built our excellent reputation because no one stays in those little neat rectangles that we draw on the charts. I sure don't want people wondering if its their job before they take action or fix a problem. I like the story of the little boy who saw a hole in the dike, stuck his finger in the hole and kept it there all night until he was relieved and engineers showed up to fix it. You can just imagine how things would have gone if the boy had started reporting the problem through channels and the city fathers had called a special meeting to investigate the boy's report. By morning the whole town would have been adrift in the Zuider Zee.

As I discuss informal team processes in this chapter the reader should keep in mind two qualities of these processes. First they are informal. Second, they are so interrelated that often they are all going on at the same time in a single conversation between team members or a single action of the team.

I have called the four key team processes in the Model for Superior Team Development and Performance 'informal' to distinguish them from the formal systems that organizations and work units use to structure and control their work. No one needs to obtain permission to use them. They are not governed by rules and regulations. You will not find them described in an organization's policies and practices manual. They do not follow some predictable pattern. No one is told when and when not to use them. You will not find any team training programmes that directly address these processes. They are part of the day-to-day work of superior teams. They reflect the norms that the team has established and which members instinctively follow. First of all, these processes are informal, but they are also very interrelated and interdependent.

When team members are in easy touch and communication is open and free, they are typically responding and adapting to an issue or problem and influencing an outcome. The routine process of showing appreciation is only possible when people are in contact and know at first hand what their peers are doing and contributing.

Communicating and contacting

Superior team members are informal in the way they communicate and interact. You will have difficulty assigning titles and levels of authority to these members by how they dress or where they eat or how they deport themselves. Conversations are free of pretence and self-serving nonsense. People acquire status through their work and their ideas and not through something as unrelated to performance as dress or position. Such informality naturally gives rise to a good bit of humour and friendly banter. It is typical in superior teams for everyone to use first names. This does not mean, of course, that superior teams are social clubs. The purpose of contact and communication is to get the job done.

Some examples of the kinds of remarks that I have recorded from people who described the process of communication and contact are:

- 'Nobody stood on ceremony. From the project manager, right down to the people who swept the shop floors, everybody used first names. We had people with all kinds of titles and degrees, but you couldn't tell who was leading and who was following from the way we talked and acted.'

- 'If you needed to see anybody about anything, you didn't go through channels or get permission. You just went and talked to the person that had the information you wanted or the expertise to help you.'

- 'Our supervisor was everywhere. He knew exactly what was going on all the time. No matter what kind of problem you had, he seemed to already know about it. It really made a big difference not to have to explain over and over again what I was doing and the kinds of roadblocks I kept running into.'

- 'Before we got started really trying to be a team, we never got any information about what other people were doing or what was happening that would affect us. We were all treated like mushrooms. But we really turned things around when we started doing things like having regular crew meetings and status meetings. Everything got better. We got to know each other better and we started helping each other a lot more. Before I got transferred it was the best team I've ever worked on.'

Thoughts while improving communication and contacting

When teams begin to focus on improving the informal process of communicating and contacting they should keep in mind two issues or conditions which influence the development and successful use of this process. These considerations are:

- Never underestimate the difficulty in creating free, open and easy communication and contact in a team. Informal communication and contact are often not the norm in work units and there may be considerable resistance to such a process.
- The process of communicating and contacting can only affect a team's performance when it is a quality process, i.e., people have the requisite interpersonal communication skills.

Resistances to informal communication and contact

From my experience in working directly with many managerial teams and work teams and from my experience in conducting seminars on team development, I have confirmed many times over that one great inhibitor to team effectiveness is the fear and distrust that people have of informal contact and communication.

A couple of years back, I made a presentation to one of NASA's senior executive teams on continuous improvement and team development. Throughout the presentation, no one spoke or responded to what I had to say except the senior official. The interaction followed this pattern: I would make some statement and then the senior official would nod agreement or he would express some exception using some tired aphorism or irrelevancy like 'there's nothing new about that', or 'we still have too many people who don't want to work', or 'the manager's job is to tell people what to do and then see that they do it'. Try as I might, I could get none of his staff to become involved in the conversation. The senior official was in the process of making some important decisions that would affect the whole organization and not one member of his staff was prepared to risk an opinion.

I was hardly surprised when I later overheard one senior manager say to his deputy, 'If you ever take my place at a staff meeting with the chief, don't you ever tell him about any problems we are having'.

Candour is built upon frequent informal conversations in which the risk of being truthful is tested over and over again. Teams and organizations pay an enormous price in productivity and quality when people are afraid to give their opinions, offer alternatives, admit to problems and propose new ideas.

One of the less insightful questions that I am sometimes asked is: 'Don't you think that it is possible for people to communicate too much and that people can have too much information?' What I find lies behind such questions are various kinds of myths and misconceptions like:

- If you give people too much information it will just upset them or make them worry. (*This kind of thinking suggests the myth that it is better not to tell a patient that he or she is going to die soon so the patient will not get upset.*)
- People need to concentrate on their jobs and not about what is going on around them. (*It is just this kind of wrong thinking that is a significant inhibitor to team development and improved organizational performance.*)
- If I am honest with other people, they might just start being honest with me. (*And, of course, it is precisely the large number of unexamined ideas, decisions and management practices that makes organizations uncompetitive.*)
- If people really want to know something then its their job to find it out.

One of the great inhibitors of efficient and effective work is that people feel obliged to calculate what it is safe to say. I think that we have only the slightest notion of the amount of wasted effort and time that go into the business of people working out what they can tell their leaders and peers or, even, what questions are safe to ask.

Every time I run a seminar for managers on topics like successful confrontation, I invariably get questions like these:

- 'How can you help your boss make a good decision when he has already made up his mind and really isn't prepared to look at any more alternatives?'
- 'How can I tell a peer the real truth and risk hurting his feelings?'
- 'How can I tell my boss that he is out of touch and really doesn't know what is going on in the shops any more?'

One way to calibrate just how 'career limiting' it can be to give one's unvarnished opinion or to provide timely information (no matter how necessary it is) is to look at the amount of time organizations devote to training their managers how to negotiate or how to influence others. When people in organizations or work units feel they cannot be candid and speak the truth (as they see it) then organizations must spend training budgets in the totally unproductive enterprise of teaching people the totally unproductive behaviour of how to become skilled in verbal manipulation.

One consideration that teams should keep in mind as they start working to improve the informal process of communicating and contacting is that such improvement can be extremely difficult because truthfulness is often not the norm in most work units and organizations. A second consideration is that communication and contact, to have a positive impact on a team's performance, necessitate high levels of interpersonal competency.

Communication and contact need skills

Managing by walking around (MBWA) has gained considerable publicity and popularity over the past few years. Involvement, a related idea, has been made popular through the current emphasis on total quality management and continuous improvement. Neither MBWA, involvement, or any other form of informal communication and contact will work, however, unless they are *quality* interactions.

The simple fact is that communication and contact can be negative processes as well as positive ones. For some jobholders, having their leaders walk around is not a useful experience. What the jobholders get too often from contact with their leaders are reprimands, unsolicited feedback, untimely interruptions and rejection of their ideas.

Often team members are not aggressive in getting the opinions of their peers on ideas and plans because of the negative and unhelpful responses they typically receive. Informal communication and contact must be a quality process, and quality is a function of skill.

In Chapter 6, I briefly discussed interpersonal problem-solving skills in connection with describing various special team competencies that are required for superior team development and performance. The two key characteristics that I associated with effective problem-solving were respect and mutuality. These are characteristics that apply to any serious conversation. They must characterize all informal communication within teams for communication to have a positive impact on performance.

There are a number of skills that are necessary for successful conversations. I have covered these skills in considerable detail in earlier publications and will not repeat that information here (Kinlaw, 1989, 1990, 1993, 1996). When teams become serious about improving the process of communicating and contacting, they can consult these or similar resources.

Quality interactions and conversations, as I have already suggested, are characterized by respect and mutuality. They also have at least one other characteristic. They develop useful information. Team members must have the skill to develop relevant, task-focused information. As they listen and respond to each other they must be able to focus on plans, actions, events and data. The purposes in all such conversations are outcomes like developing information, improving understanding, corroborating judgements, verifying data and the like. To develop relevant information means:

- creating no barriers to the other person's input
- stimulating the other person to input information.

It is particularly difficult for a team member to listen to news that presents that member with problems and issues that he/she is not expecting or runs counter to the member's perceptions. It is not easy for team members to listen to opinions that force them to devalue their own.

Skilled listening is, of course, the key to developing information successfully. Skilled listening has at least these elements:

1   The ability to receive accurately the whole message sent by another person, i.e., the entire verbal, non-verbal and emotional content of a message.
2   The ability to convey to another person by one's own verbal and non-verbal behaviour that one is listening.
3   The ability to encourage another person to continue to speak and build information.

These three elements largely depend on the mental skill to listen without prematurely evaluating what the other person is saying. Most often we add our own mental comments to the messages that we receive. We note the degree to which we think that what we have heard is true or false, right or wrong, accurate or inaccurate, etc. When we listen evaluatively, therefore, we are listening very much to ourselves – to our own mental comments as part of the message we are receiving. We are not, therefore, concentrating on just listening and understanding what the other person is saying. When we listen evaluatively, of course, we tend to act evaluatively and convey judgement or disbelief to the other person – rather than just conveying our understanding.

A second consideration that teams should keep in mind as they plan to improve the process of informal communicating and contacting is that this process, to be successful, must be a quality process. To make it a quality process the team members must have highly developed interpersonal communication skills that permit them consistently to:

● convey respect
● maintain mutuality
● develop useful information.

The first informal process that is characteristic of superior teams is communicating and contacting. The second process is responding and adapting.

Responding and adapting

Superior teams refuse to be stymied. They view problems as opportunities. They expect team members to take the initiative to respond to problems and issues as they develop, and they join forces easily to respond to changes that affect the whole team. They expect team members to give immediate attention to requests for assistance from each other.

Some of the specific kinds of behaviours that are characteristic of superior teams and which illustrate the practical meaning of being responsive and adaptive are that team members:

- obtain immediate help on priority work problems
- receive serious consideration for suggestions to improve any aspect of the teams's performance
- have ready access to anyone who can help them complete their jobs
- receive quick responses from their supervisors to help them resolve personal problems that impact on their work
- can obtain a prompt decision when they need it.

A supervisor in a telephone company told me a story a few years ago that illustrates just what responsiveness and adaptability can mean.

We had been told that we would be moving sometime in the near future to a new building that had been built across town. But every time we would get a date, it would change. After a while we just put the hold thing in the back of our minds. In fact, it got to be a kind of joke among the operators. Guys started saying things to each other in the morning like, 'Hey, Charlie, you still here, I thought you moved,' or 'You want to join our lottery? You have to pick which will come first, the move or your retirement.' I can't tell you how many times we packed and unpacked. Then, it happens. We get the word on a Thursday that we have to move and be up and running on the following Monday. Also, we're told that we can't turn off the machines until the end of the working day on Thursday. To be on such a short fuse was bad enough, but just add to that things like we got short changed on the number of trucks we needed. We had a gate lift break on the back of a truck with a large memory component on it. We get to the new facility and discover that the electricians haven't finished their job. We ended up using some of our own pickups, borrowing some heavy duty jacks from a house-moving outfit, running our own cables and doing only God knows what. But when 7.30 rolled around on Monday morning we were on line. How the hell we did it I still don't really know. But I can tell you one thing, that was one proud and tired outfit.

Thoughts while improving responding and adapting

Responsiveness and adaptability are fundamental to superior performance. When teams consider improving this process, there are at least two considerations that they should remember. First, as with communicating and contacting, people have often developed habits and mind sets that resist the idea of responsiveness. Second, to create high levels of responsiveness and adaptability the process has to be reinforced over and over again.

Resistances

I was serving recently as a consultant to a staff group that had the responsibility to take action on data provided from a survey that had been conducted by corporate headquarters. The survey had taken up a considerable amount of employee time and had cost a great deal of money. During my work with the staff I learned at first hand just how strong the habits of not being responsive and adaptive can become.

I was first commissioned to analyse the study and then identify implications of the study that were unambiguous and which suggested improvement opportunities for the organization. I was told that it was imperative that I complete my analysis and make a presentation to this staff group within seven days. My report was delivered on time. It was accepted. The presentation that I was supposed to give has never happened. The staff has long since missed the opportunity to act on the information from the survey. My later conversations with the group indicate that no one remembers that there was a need for quick response. To date, as far as I know, nothing has been done to use the survey data. What apparently happened was that this staff group initially thought the survey was important and should be taken seriously. After it had commissioned me to do my analysis, the group made a presentation to senior management about the survey and what the staff was doing to act on the findings. Senior management responded negatively to the staff group's presentation. Members of the group later reacted by dropping its interest in the survey and setting aside the data. No attempt was made to regroup and find new strategies to work around the roadblocks that they had encountered with senior management.

I have conducted hundreds of training programmes over the years in a very wide range of private and public organizations. I have, sad to say, observed at first hand the lack of responsiveness and adaptability that training offices too often exhibit.

I remember one training office in which each training programme was assigned to a separate co-ordinator. And 'separate' was really the operative word. If I had even the simplest question about a programme, like where it would be held, or on what dates it was scheduled, it was absolutely impossible to get that information unless the person directly responsible for that programme was available. If the person that I needed to talk to was on leave or sick, I could never get the information I required. No one in that training office expected help from a colleague and no one asked for help.

Early in my consulting career (before I discovered that to survive I should never assume that certain clients would take care of even the minimum preparations for a training event) I had the following repetitive experiences.

I arrive at the designated training room 30 minutes before the programme is scheduled to start. The door to the training room is locked. Participants are standing in the hall waiting to get in. I start trying to find a person to find the key. I learn that the person who is responsible for the programme will not be in this day. The key is that person's responsibility. No one else on the training staff has any idea how to help or any inclination to help. I personally find the building superintendent or someone from maintenance and get the door open. I start the programme an hour late and only the participants and myself seem to care.

Another repetitive experience goes like this. I arrive at a training room. This time the door is open, but the room is a mess. Trash cans are full, tables have not been set up, chairs are stacked and none of the equipment is present that was promised by the client. I contact my programme co-ordinator. I am told that the room was supposed to have been set up the night before, but another programme co-ordinator scheduled an evening class and there had not been time to get a cleaning crew in to take care of the room. I am also told that the overhead projector was ordered but for some reason was not delivered. As I observe the staff it is clear that no one else is going to help my programme co-ordinator. No one else feels the slightest responsibility for the group's image or its total performance.

When there is a lack of internal responsiveness in a work unit (as in the case of all the other informal processes) the total performance of the unit suffers. There is no quick or easy way to improve a team's internal responsiveness when habits of not responding have become thoroughly entrenched.

Lack of responsiveness and adaptability have a number of sources. Here are a few possibilities:

1   People are told to do their own jobs and are held responsible only for doing their own jobs. They never get acknowledged or rewarded for helping someone else. They only get fussed at when they do not do what they have been told to do. Over the years a myopic focus on one's own job has been rewarded and reinforced.

2   To take any kind of quick action may entail too much risk. People are not sure just how many degrees of freedom they have. They worry about breaking some rule or violating some precedent.

3   People in work units may have a strong sense of being in competition with each other. They may develop the perception that they can only succeed through the failures of their colleagues.

The resistances to being responsive to each other may have become part of a work unit's climate. To create high levels of responsiveness and adaptability will, in such cases, require nothing short of changing the unit's work climate. What this means largely, of course, is changing the unit's norms. Changing norms will never occur quickly or easily. This leads me to the second strategic consideration that affects improving responsiveness and adaptability. It can usually be done only through continuous reinforcement.

Reinforcing the process

Continuous attention and reinforcement is needed to develop high levels of responsiveness. I know of a supervisor who has developed a set of values in his team that he communicates and discusses with each new person that joins his team. Among the various values that this supervisor talks about are:

- Never bring a problem to me unless you have obtained all the help you can from your other team members to solve it.
- Never refuse help to anybody when they ask for it.
- Never bring a problem to me unless you have devised at least three different ways to solve it.

In another team, at each team meeting, the first question that is asked is 'Who needs help with anything?' The follow-up question is 'Who can help?'

One highly innovative approach that a team took after attending a team development workshop of mine was to establish a monthly 'slam dunk' award and their 'assists' award. These terms, of course, come from the game of basketball. The slam dunk is given to the team member or members who bring the greatest direct credit on the team by solving a problem or taking care of a special need of a customer. The assist award is given to the member or members who provide the most help to another team member during the month. Any team member can nominate any other team member or members for these awards and the whole team makes the final decisions. From the time new employees enter this team they begin to learn about the importance of responsiveness and adaptability. And the importance of the process is reinforced every time an assist award is given out.

A team leader that I worked with a few years ago became quite concerned about how many times he said 'no' when he was asked for help and the impact that kind of modelling had on the rest of the team. He got the idea of placing two small boxes on his desk. One box was labelled 'yes' and the other was labelled 'no'. Every time a person asked for assistance and he said 'yes' he put a green chip in the 'yes' box. Every time he said 'no' he put a red chip in the 'no' box. He later told me that his technique had really put him under pressure to say 'yes' and had made a big difference in his own responsiveness.

Responsiveness and adaptability is one of the key informal processes that supports superior team performance. When teams begin to look at ways to improve this process, there are at least two considerations that they should remember. First, people have often developed habits and mind sets that lead them to resist being responsive and adaptive. Second, to create high levels of responsiveness and adaptability the process has to be reinforced over and over again.

We have now looked at two informal processes that superior teams employ to support their overall effectiveness: communicating and contacting, and responding and adapting. The next process that I will examine is influencing and improving.

Influencing and improving

The continuous, incremental improvements that take place in a team are a function of all the informal processes. All four processes of communicating and contacting, responding and adapting, influencing and improving, and appreciating and celebrating strengthen the other elements in the Model for Superior Team Development and Performance. It is clear, however, that creating opportunities for influence plays a special role in a team's development and performance because these opportunities are the means of releasing and using the competencies of team members.

In Chapter 6, I discussed how the competencies of a team can be fully used and developed. One point I made was that a person must have the chance to demonstrate a competency and must feel confident to demonstrate a competency in order for that person to be perceived as competent. Underlying the process of being competent, then, is the opportunity to be *influential*.

In another book of mine, *The Practice of Empowerment* (Kinlaw, 1995), I have developed the relationship between influence and competence and provided an extensive analysis of why this relationship must exist in organizations which want to make the most of their human resources. I will not repeat that analysis here. Figure 7.1, Influence process and pay-offs, does, however, give a simple and graphic display of the relationship between influence, competencies and pay-offs for the team. By extending opportunities for influence teams tap more and more of their member's competencies. As competencies are used, members seek more opportunities to be influential. The more opportunities they acquire to be influential, the more competencies they will develop in order to be more influential. And so on and on the process goes. The pay-offs from people being influential have now been well documented. The typical results are better quality, better development of people and continuous improvement (Cleland, 1996; Kinlaw, 1995; Lawler, 1986; Werther, 1981).

Thoughts while improving influencing and improving

Three useful considerations that teams can keep in mind as they begin to strengthen their informal process of influencing and improving are:

- There can be strong resistances to extending influence.
- Influence should always be coupled clearly with improvement.
- Influencing and improving should be considered as a way of life and not as a programme.

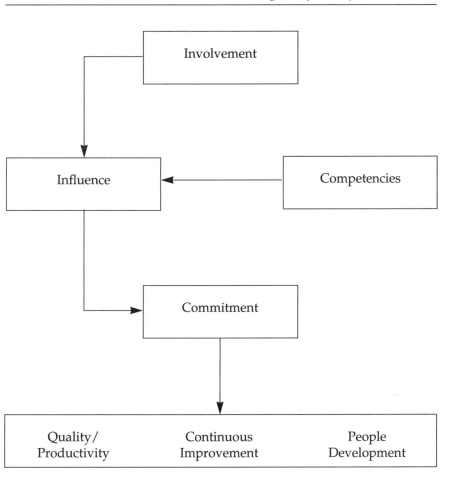

Figure 7.1 Influence process and pay-offs

Resistances

Although extending influence to people has produced demonstrable positive results and although most supervisors believe
that strengthening employee influence is a good thing (Klein,
1984), there are also a number of deep-seated resistances to
extending influence to people. When teams decide to work on
the degree of influence of their members, they can expect to run
up against resistances caused by one or more of the following:

- doubts about people's motivation and competence
- fear that people who think they have control will lose it
- lack of confidence in leaders about their own competency
- the perception that giving people influence will mean more work for leaders
- the notion that to give people more influence will cost everybody more time
- the general fear of uncertainty and instability.

All of these resistances have in common two difficulties. First, they reflect some fear of the unknown. Second, they reflect some doubt about personal pay-off. Every time I have started a team development process with work units I have found people asking the same kinds of questions:

- 'What will I be expected to do? Will I be expected to do something that I don't know how to do?'
- 'What is the pay-off? Am I going to be rewarded if I become more influential and help others become more influential?'

I have already stated that the only way to develop a team is through teamwork. Work units that begin to develop themselves into fully functioning teams all go through a 'proof of concept phase'. They grow into teams as they begin to function as teams. Being influential and extending influence are essential attributes of a team and are precisely what work units begin to do more and more of as they develop themselves into teams.

The only way to dispel the various myths associated with the process of influencing, and the only way to overcome the resistances that members of teams may have to becoming more influential, is for teams to make increasing influence a specific target and for the team to manage the matter of influence themselves. One way to help a team to extend the influence of its members and that of the team as a whole is for the team to use a set of questions to help it plan its intentions to extend influence and a set of indicators that it can use to determine if it is being successful in its intentions. Here is a set of questions that some teams have used:

1 What blocks now exist that keep individual members from being more influential on the team?
2 What can the team do to remove these blocks?
3 What blocks now exist that keep the whole team from being more influential as a team?
4 What can the team do to remove these blocks?
5 When our team is successful in extending the influence of its members, what changes in the behaviours of members should we expect?
6 When our team is successful in extending the influence of the team as a whole, what changes in the way the team does business with its internal and external suppliers and customers should we expect?

A second consideration for teams to keep in mind while improving the process of influencing and improving is that such improvements should always be clearly coupled with improving performance.

Coupling influence with improvement

The business of improving the process of influencing has an intensely practical purpose. The purpose is to ensure that the team continues to perform at its highest level of potential. This means, of course, that the team must always be on a positive improvement slope.

Who knows most about the task being performed? Obviously, it is the person who has experience in performing it. Who is most likely to have the best information about how to improve the performance of a task? Obviously, it is the person who performs it. Who is most likely to have the best information about work flow processes? Obviously, it is the people who use it day in and day out. Who can most likely improve a work process? Obviously, it is the people who use it.

This litany of questions and answers can be extended to every aspect of a team's performance. Stimulating and encouraging people to be influential (let us never forget) is simply the practical way to make the fullest use of the competencies that team members have.

The template against which every initiative for extending influence should be compared is quality. The goal should be that every team member is expected to take whatever action is necessary to improve the quality of ideas, of decisions, of problem-solving, of work processes and of production itself. Extending influence means that people are expected to stop an assembly line when errors or defects are discovered. It means that no change in a job task or work process is made unless the change has been tested and passed by the people it affects.

When teams deal with the process of influencing, they should keep clearly before them exactly what they are intending. The goal is not democracy or equality. The goal is always continuous improvement.

Teams can expect that one of the primary resistances to their gaining more influence will be the leaders in the organization. When I work with organizations to help them move to a team-centred structure, the kinds of statements that I fully expect to hear from leaders are:

- 'I always give my people a chance to comment on what I'm planning to do, it makes them feel like they have a say even when I have already made up my mind.'
- 'I get paid to make decisions. I'm the one who is held responsible. I don't mind getting input from people, but when I know what's best, then that's what we are going to do.'
- 'People in this unit can have as much influence as they want. The fact is that they don't want it. I'm their supervisor and they expect me to tell them what to do.'
- 'Each of us has a job to do. We are all good at our jobs. If we started checking with each other about what we planned to do, nothing would ever get done around here.'

Influence and improvement as a way of life
Influencing and improving, in superior teams, are a way of life. On superior teams, no one is expected to accept automatically ideas or changes, without serious questioning and analysis. No one is expected to just 'go along' in order to 'get along'. Superior teams are fields of energetic conflict. The norm is for each team

member to use fully all of his/her mental resources. Every person is an active member.

Within the larger organization the influence that teams exert must become as commonplace as the influence team members exert on their teams. This means, of course, that influence cannot become some sort of special programme, like total quality or process improvement or re-engineering.

Formal programmes are probably necessary just to get people's attention and to help organizations target the use of their resources. We should always keep in mind, however, that formal programmes have serious limitations.

The trouble with programmes is that they are programmes. Just the idea of programmes carries a lot of negative baggage. Programmes are often viewed like the latest car sale. Not many people take seriously the overstated claims of each new car sale. No one truly believes that 'this is the sale of the century', or that 'this is the lowest price anywhere', or 'name your own price because every car must go'.

Special programmes in organizations, like car sales, have a credibility problem. Programmes also tend to direct people towards short-term goals and pay-offs. It becomes easy, therefore, to abandon programmes when the pay-offs are not forthcoming.

There are four informal processes which are very characteristic of superior teams. Thus far I have described three of these processes: communicating and contacting, responding and adapting, and influencing and improving. The final process is appreciating and celebrating.

Appreciating and celebrating

There can be no question that the members of superior teams are aware of their own value and that they are quite clear about the contributions that they make to the team's success. This sense of clear personal value is the result of a highly visible and dynamic process of appreciating and celebrating (Kinlaw, 1989, 1996a, 1997).

Appreciating and celebrating are expressed through two channels; one is formal and the other is informal. Both channels must be fully used simply because appreciating and celebrating are linked directly to a team's development and performance. People need promotions, bonuses, citations and other formal awards. Formal awards, however, do have a number of limitations and formal awards cannot, by themselves, communicate to team members their full value.

Formal awards have a number of limitations. First, their impact is often diluted because they are not timely. By the time they are received, the events which they commemorate may have long passed. I have heard many stories from people who describe how their awards did not mean much because, by the time the award was received, the person receiving the award had moved on to another job or the population of their work unit had changed. Awards clearly lose a lot of their impact when they are received among strangers.

A second limitation of formal awards is that they may not, in fact, communicate appreciation. I know of a number of organizations that have 'employee of the month' programmes. I also know that many employees do not feel it is an honour to be the employee of the month. They feel that reward is 'passed around' or they feel that managers at the last minute are told to identify a candidate. Aboard some US Navy ships one of the worst things that can happen to a crew member is to be made 'sailor of the month'. The fear is that other sailors will view the recipient as ingratiating.

Another example that comes to mind to illustrate how formal awards can sometimes not be appreciated by recipients concerns an engineering achievement award given by a Californian company. The award was given to an individual who had made the most significant contribution to the success of some engineering project delivered to a customer. The problem was that the person singled out for the award always felt very self-conscious because he or she felt that it was inappropriate to accept an award that really should have gone to all the people who had worked on the project.

A final limitation to the formal systems that organizations and teams use to acknowledge the importance and contributions of team members is that these systems are rarely fully utilized. This is especially the case in large organizations.

There are at least two reasons that I have identified which contribute to this lack of use. First, leaders who are required to initiate action for awards often do not know about all the awards that are available. Second, formal awards usually involve a good bit of paperwork and supervisors and other leaders may choose to avoid what they consider 'extra' work.

One additional observation about formal and informal systems is that informal awards are likely to have more impact on people than formal ones. When I have asked jobholders to tell me about something that happened to them that made them feel especially appreciated and valued by their organizations, more than 85 per cent of the time they have identified some informal action or event.

Here is an example of what people tell me. A woman in a seminar of mine described the following experience.

I was a secretary at the time and had gone out of my way to help a group of mechanics who were responsible for the four tie-down posts that keep the Shuttle stable on the pad until the moment the engines are turned on. One afternoon I received a telephone call from the shop where these mechanics worked and was told that there was an emergency and would I please come down. I dropped everything and rushed down to the shop. When I walked in the door the mechanics were lined up with their large torque wrenches held up making an archway like the ones you see at military weddings. Only, of course, they use swords. I walked through the arch of wrenches to the end of the shop. They had set a table with a beautiful cake and had got a little combo (from who knows where) that was playing music. When I got through the arch, the music stops and all the mechanics gather round. Then one of them steps forward and presents me with a sash (like the ones you see in a beauty contest). The sash reads 'Ms. Tie-Down Post of 1985'. I can tell you that it was an experience that probably means more to me than anything that has ever happened to me at work.

A recent participant in a residential manager education programme of mine gave me the following example of another creative informal award.

Our software manager had a thing about penquins. He had pictures of penquins of every kind posted all over his office. In one of
our meetings we got on the crazy idea of penquins wearing those
surfing trunks called 'jams'. Later on while I was walking through
a store I saw a stuffed doll of Opus, the penquin in the cartoon.
The doll had on a beach hat and sandals. As I looked at the doll the
idea pops into my mind to create an award for the software folks
and pass it around each month to the top programmer. I named it
on the spot the 'Penquin Jam' award and bought the doll and a
pair of jams for it. The way we finally set it up was that the person
who got the award had to add something personal to it each time.
If you can believe it, the 'Penquin Jam' is one that people on my
team really prize. It has become a real tradition.

Appreciating and celebrating is a process that is obvious in
superior teams. As teams go about strengthening this process
there are a few considerations that they should keep in mind.

Thoughts while improving the process of appreciating and celebrating

The following considerations can help teams as they begin to
strengthen the informal process of appreciating and acknowledging:

- Do not forget that there is more to celebrate than superior
  performance.
- Do not be afraid of doing too much.
- Consider the team.

There is more to appreciate and celebrate than perfor-mance

One great advantage of informal acts of appreciation is that they
can do more than just acknowledge superior performance. They

can acknowledge people who show up day after day and do routine jobs that are not spectacular or even visible. They can tell people how courageous they are just for showing up. They can communicate special thanks when people patiently put up with bureaucratic delay and hostile customers and insensitive leaders.

Nobody shows much interest in tap water until it stops running. People usually take little interest in the grass around their buildings until they observe that it has not been cut. As long as the people in accounting and payroll deliver the pay cheques on time, they are rarely singled out for special praise.

When teams think about improving the process of appreciating and celebrating, they should consider much more than just performance. They should work out how to become more sensitive to people who do the dirty jobs and the routine jobs. They should start celebrating the triumphs of patience that people make when they persevere in the face of bureaucratic delay and inertia.

You cannot do too much

In the various surveys that I have conducted over the past few years of organizations and work teams, the three most serious problems that I have identified are that jobholders believe that:

- their organizations and teams do not have clear improvement goals and objectives
- that people have insufficient influence over their jobs, their work units and their total organizations
- they do not feel sufficiently appreciated and valued by their work units organizations.

In all the workshops and seminars that I have conducted and in all the direct contacts that I have with hundreds of work units, I have never run into the problem that people felt that they were thanked too often. Some people do, however, have the odd notion that 'you can thank people too much' or 'you can overdo this business of appreciation'.

Based on my own experience, I would like to challenge any team to overdo appreciating and celebrating the importance and value of team members. Having never seen such a phenomenon, I very much like to observe it at first hand. *We know that too little appreciation affects performance negatively. We have not the slightest hint that too much appreciation has a negative impact on performance.*

Consider the team

The process of appreciating and celebrating is a very powerful tool for developing superior teams. For it to be such a powerful tool the team must consider the team more than individuals. Individual awards and celebrations are important. It is team success and performance which must have the highest priority. In the organizations with which I have consulted over the past 15 years there is almost a ten to one ratio of individual to team awards. And this ratio only reflects what goes on in formal systems. I imagine the difference between the frequency of individual to team awards would be even greater if I had considered informal awards.

I have now discussed two of the four primary elements in the Model for Superior Team Development and Performance, results and processes. In the next chapter I will describe in detail the third element in the model, feelings.

8 Focusing on feelings

In the two previous chapters I have discussed two of the primary elements in the Model for Superior Team Development and Performance: results and processes. In this chapter I will discuss a set of feelings which form a third primary element in the model.

One of the simplest and most direct ways that I have found to describe superior teams is that their members consistently describe a set of personal feelings which are qualitatively different from the feelings that members of poor or average teams describe. These feelings are as persistent as they are pervasive.

Members of superior teams do, of course, experience at times the same negative feelings that members of any work unit have. Sometimes they feel put upon, frustrated and angry. At other times they feel unhappy, anxious and despondent. What is so distinctive about superior teams, however, is that negative feelings do not persist. These feelings find resolution and become generally overpowered by positive feelings.

Members of superior teams talk about their feelings in a language that is both energetic and colourful. A member of a lagging crew put it this way:

161

People used to ask me how the hell I could enjoy such dirty work. I guess I never thought of it as dirty. I sure never felt sorry for myself. How the hell could I? There wasn't a guy in my crew that ever ducked a tough job or sat on their butts letting somebody else do the work. We were really tight. I can't say that I liked all of the other guys. There were some I wouldn't want to take home or anything like that. But I've never worked with a better crew before or since.

A sales representative described his feelings in a conversation with me as follows:

You couldn't help but feel part of a team. We were so focused on out-selling our competitors that we didn't have time to fight with each other. We even had a sign in our conference room that read 'The enemy is not your buddy, it's the competition'.

From our analysis of the data from our original study, we were able to identify five feelings which were consistently experienced by members of superior teams. After five years of experience and further study, I still conclude that these five feelings remain dominant in the experience of superior teams. These feelings are:

- inclusion
- commitment
- loyalty
- pride
- trust.

Inclusion

Among the kinds of words and phrases of the members of teams that I recorded in the initial study and which have been confirmed many times over are:

- We all felt we belonged.
- We were concerned about each other, on and off the job.
- We were close.

- I felt accepted.
- I felt I was important.
- I always knew what was going on.
- People took me seriously.
- I was respected.
- We all knew we had a part when the team succeeded.

In superior teams there are no first-, second- or third-class citizens. Some of the actions or conditions that create a sense of inclusion are:

- Team members get the information that affects their job and their life in the organization.
- The right team members attend the right meetings.
- Team members have a say when decisions are made that affect them.
- New ideas are encouraged and treated with respect.
- Team members have a fair chance at challenging work.
- High levels of appreciation are expressed to team members for their value to the team.
- Team members receive quick response from other team members when they ask for help.
- Team members exhibit a practical concern for each other's well-being.
- People have the chance to demonstrate their full competence.
- Team members all participate in a variety of social activities.

Symbols are powerful tools to create inclusion or subvert inclusion. A contractor friend of mine told me the following story.

I have had a number of the same clients for many, many years. The managers in one of my client organizations have told me on a number of occasions that they considered me as part of the team because I was a person who was trusted by everyone and that people knew that I would never betray a confidence. Sometimes when I get a new contract or purchase order I have a little trouble believing that I am really part of the team, however, because the first word that jumps out at me is 'vendor'. I always somehow picture a vendor as a guy standing on a street corner turning an organ-grinder with a monkey on his shoulder with a tin cup begging for handouts.

I very much agree with Ricardo Semler, President of Semco, who maintains that among the biggest enemies of performance are managers who are jealous of their power and prerogatives (Semler, 1989). I extend the problem of prerogatives beyond managers to include the whole workforce. Prerogatives of any kind (no matter who benefits from them) must have a clearly functional reason for existing to serve the purposes of team development. When anyone gets special treatment on a team, the reason for the treatment must be obviously connected to the person's performance and value to the team.

Aboard ship when the on-coming watch goes to the head of the food queue, the reason is obvious to everyone. The on-coming watch must be fed in order to relieve the section that is currently on watch. Most privileges, however, have no such obviously functional value.

The practice of reserved parking, for example, has very little to commend it. The message is that the people who have reserved parking places are more important than those who do not. Every single day that a worker hunts around to find a place to park and must drive past all the spaces that are reserved for managers, supervisors and staff personnel, that worker gets a clear lesson in relative importance.

One misguided practice of companies that I find fascinating is that they select an 'employee of the month' and then give the winner a reserved parking place for one month. The message is that the people who do the work must do something special to get a reserved spot for even a month while members of the hierarchy get their spots without ever doing anything special to earn them.

I listened with disbelief once while two senior managers discussed their concern that 'engineers don't act like engineers, they don't seem to be conscious that they are professionals, when you see them on the flight processing floor you can't tell them from the technicians'. As I listened I kept thinking of a movie I had seen recently. The movie was a comedy and one of the funniest scenes occurs when one worker is indoctrinating a new worker into the culture of the organization. The new worker is told that the most important thing to keep in mind was the distinction in the organization between the 'suits' and the 'non-suits'. The rule was that non-suits (the workers) never, under any circumstance, spoke to the suits (management) unless the suits spoke first.

Inclusion is created and maintained by both functional and symbolic aspects of a team's environment. What teams must remember is that their members must feel a strong sense of inclusion if the team is to continue to develop and reach sustained levels of superior performance. Teams ensure that people are treated with respect, that they have a chance to demonstrate their competence etc. Teams must also be sensitive to the symbols which suggest inclusion and those that reinforce the sense of hierarchy and degrees of importance and value.

The first feeling that is characteristic of superior teams is inclusion. The second is commitment.

Commitment

People on superior teams describe themselves as:

- focused
- looking forward to going to work
- caring about results and how well the team did
- taking it quite personally when the team did not meet its goals
- making personal sacrifices to make sure the team succeeded
- determined to succeed
- single-minded
- never giving up.

In my books on coaching (Kinlaw, 1989, 1996, 1997) I suggested that there are at least two easily recognized indicators to determine just how committed people are. The first is the degree to which people are goal-oriented, and the second indicator is the degree of sacrifice that people are willing to make to reach the goal. These two indicators are clearly evident in the many stories and comments that I have collected from people as they described their experiences on superior teams.

The lead mechanic in an air compressor team gave this colourful description of his present experience in his shop:

When you show up for work in our shop, you had better have your pants hitched up and your shoes laced. We mean business and that's no ... When our shop got organized, the whole ... operation was in a whole lot of hurt. Within one year we achieved a rate of zero down time for air supply to every building and we haven't had a single tool fail in any shop because it didn't have air.

Superior teams achieve their superior levels of performance through commitment. Other kinds of work units struggle to maintain barely satisfactory levels of performance through control. Commitment to quality by every single person who touches a process, a product or a service is the only proven way to ensure outputs that are 100 per cent fit to use, 100 per cent of the time. No organization has ever shown that such a level of quality could be achieved by quality inspectors and engineers. There is simply no contest between teams that develop commitment in their members and those work units that depend on the grudging compliance of members to achieve results.

A second feeling that is typical of members of superior teams is commitment. A third is loyalty.

Loyalty

I have used commitment to capture the many different ways that members of superior teams describe the way they feel about the team's goals, objectives and priorities. I have selected the term loyalty to capture the way members describe their feelings toward each other. Some typical expressions are:

● I think we really cared what happened to each other.
● We depended on each other so much, you just had to take

care of your buddies, there was no other way you could get the job done.

- We had such a reputation that we could get the very best people to work in our shop. We just started out with the best and that's how we always thought of each other.
- Nobody tried to show anybody else up. The old hands were really good about helping the new guys learn the ropes.
- I think we all operated on the assumption that if anybody screwed up it was everybody's fault. It just never seemed important to waste time finding a fall guy.

I have seen many times over just what happens to work units when loyalty among jobholders does not exist. Take, for example, my experience in working with a security unit at a government installation some years ago.

I was contacted by management and presented with a set of their concerns and issues. Most of these were the typical sort of things that I have learned to expect, i.e., 'our supervisors aren't acting like leaders', 'our employees aren't motivated', 'our people are not sufficiently professional'. All of these statements were, of course, too general to be treated as problems. And, as is usually the case, none of these general statements even hinted at what the real problems turned out to be. The underlying problems that I was finally able to identify were:

1 Promotions and assignments were given out according to the whims and biases of the Chief of Security and other senior officers.
2 Guards were encouraged to inform on their peers and to bring their stories and complaints directly to the senior officers without first discussing their concerns with their peers.

My experience with this security unit demonstrated forcefully just how interrelated all of the feelings that are characteristic of superior teams are. Without loyalty in the unit, there was no commitment to a common set of performance goals. If there was a common goal among the rank and file it was survival. Without loyalty and commitment, there was very little trust and very little for people to feel much pride about. And with all of these feelings showing up on the negative side of the ledger, members of the unit certainly did not feel any degree of inclusion.

Loyalty in superior teams becomes visible in at least two sets of behaviours. First, members go out of their way to ensure the success of their peers. Second, members give their colleagues the benefit of the doubt when they have apparently failed to meet an obligation or fulfil a commitment.

The way members of superior teams feel about the success of their fellow team members is captured in what a member of a print shop had to say about loyalty.

I always had the feeling that my gang was truly interested in making sure we all got our jobs done. We used to joke a lot about our mistakes and mess ups. We even had a 'spilled ink' award that we presented to the person who had screwed up in some spectacular way. But underneath it all we really cared about each other. On a day-to-day basis we all went out of our way to help each other look good and get the job done.

Giving other team members the benefit of the doubt is illustrated in the following story from the leader of a team that was responsible for a large computerized inventory control system.

Our team was responsible for keeping the system up and running. So many operations depended on the system that when we had a problem it always showed up in a hurry and it was very visible to everyone. Our team had to give a status report to our division chief every morning at 7.15 a.m. If there was ever an opportunity to 'shoot the messenger' and find fault that morning review session was really it. I mean it was like being in charge of the electric lights or something. Nobody really notices so long as the lights are on. People just take it for granted. But look out if the lights go off. Then all hell breaks lose. Well, it was like that with the inventory system. It worked from our mainframe and our users were scattered all over our operating area. If the system or any part of it went down, our boss got instant feedback. At any rate, what I think has been so incredible is that our division chief has never treated us as though we set out to make the system fail. He has just always assumed that we were working our butts off to keep it going. So when something happened and we had to tell him some bad news at our 7.15 session, he would always respond by asking us to tell him what we were doing about it and ask if we needed his help in any way.

Loyalty is a feeling that is distinctive among members of superior teams. You see loyalty in action all the time on these teams. People go out of their way to ensure their colleagues' success and they assume that, when things do go wrong, their colleagues did not set out to make them go wrong. The fourth feeling that is very obvious among the members of superior teams is pride.

Pride

There are a number of specific kinds of behaviours that are visible among the members of superior teams which give clear definition to what pride means in these teams.

- Members work hard at obtaining feedback and know how they and their teams are doing at all times.
- Feedback is taken seriously as a chance to improve and is not responded to defensively.
- Members believe that what they do is important and know how their products and services are tied to the organization's goals and final outputs.
- Members participate in setting performance goals and standards for themselves and for the whole team.
- Members have a strong orientation toward the future and fully expect to exceed their own current levels of performance.
- There is a much greater emphasis on team achievement and success than on individual achievement and success.

Among the many phrases that we have recorded from superior team members that illustrate the meaning of team pride are:

- 'I felt responsible, everything about the job that went right or wrong reflected directly on me.'
- 'I felt confident. I felt like I could handle just about anything that I was asked to do.'
- 'We all felt like we really counted, like we were worth something. We just had that feeling that the whole company knew that when people came to us they were going to get a job done that was the best.'
- 'We had saved so many people's bacon so often that we had an unlimited number of chits that we could call in at any time. We could get things done faster and better than anybody else because we had developed our own private support system.'

Work and self-worth are the two factors in pride that interact with each other and tend to increase the strong sense of pride found in superior teams. We have always known that when people do something of obvious worth, they feel a strong sense of personal worth. It is a strong sense of personal worth that leads people to want to express that worth in what they do.

Superior teams are able to fuel this interaction between performance and personal worth. On superior teams, people not only have the opportunity to feel worth because of what they do as individuals, they have the chance to feel worth because they are valued members of a whole team that is performing well. A member of a section in a comptroller's office put it this way:

I actually felt important the day I was hired into the section – even before I had done anything. The whole company knew that this section could get just about anybody it wanted. There was a waiting list for any opening that might occur. And later on, when I actually began to make a contribution, I felt like I was one of the luckiest people in the company. The people in the section recognized that I was doing really good work and the whole team was recognized as something very special in the company.

I have now covered four of the key feelings associated with superior teams: inclusion, commitment, loyalty and pride. The last special feeling included in the Model for Superior Team Development and Performance is trust.

Trust

In superior teams trust has some very specific meanings. It means that members:

- will do what they say they are going to do
- are sometimes painfully straightforward and never conceal information from each other that they feel their colleagues should have
- can be depended on because they are viewed by their colleagues as having the knowledge and skills to perform
- are willing to listen to each other and to defer to each other because they expect reliable information and good ideas from each other.

The kinds of behaviours that work against trust developing on work teams are:

- People are checked up on frequently and are required to give status reports often about how they are doing or how the job is coming along.
- People feel like they are being micromanaged, decisions are made which they should make and they are given detailed direction on how to do their jobs.
- There is a general lack of communication, people are often surprised by plans, changes and problems which they should have known about.
- There is a great deal of secrecy about pay, promotions, awards, job assignments and the like.

Trust, of course, interacts with the other key feelings of inclusion, commitment, loyalty and pride. All of these feelings feed on each other. It is easy to feel included in a group of people whom one trusts. It is easy to become committed to the goals and values of an organization when we trust the people who communicate these goals and values.

Here is an example of what trust feels like in superior teams. A secretary described her relationship with her network team of company secretaries this way.

I was a secretary in the company for a good many years before the secretaries started thinking of themselves as a team. We rarely saw each other because we all worked in different parts of the company. We all did a lot of business by phone, but we largely thought of ourselves as members of teams made up of our boss and the other staff members. A couple of years ago we started taking a proactive position about ourselves and one of the first things that we did was to request some of the same kind of training that we saw managers and supervisors going to. We were especially interested in a total quality management seminar that the company was offering to work teams. We weren't a work team but we were able to get a special seminar put together on total quality management for just the secretaries. It turned out to be a tremendous team development experience. Ever since the seminar we have been meeting regularly and I can tell you that there is all the difference in the world in the way we work together. What's really different is that we have developed a lot of trust among ourselves. We have begun to appreciate all the kinds of help that we can give to each other. We go out of our way to keep each other informed about everything that goes on. We get help from each other whenever we need it. We have surprised everybody, especially our bosses, with the way we can get information and solve problems that no one else can manage. And the secret is simply that we now think of ourselves as a team and we know that we can trust each other to help when we need it.

These then are the five key feelings that are typical of superior work teams and people who have experienced superior teamwork. This list of five is certainly not an exhaustive list. These particular feelings are, however, so pervasive and predictable, that they can be used as baselines to assess team development and as targets for improving team development.

In the next section of this chapter I will discuss some considerations that teams should keep in mind as they consider strengthening these key feelings among their members.

Thoughts while strengthening key feelings

Because all of the five key feelings associated with superior teams are so closely related and interactive, it is all but impossible to influence one without influencing one or more of the others. You will find below some thoughts that can help teams as they undertake to strengthen the five feelings that are so characteristic of superior teams.

When teams consider what might be done to strengthen the key feelings that have been discussed in this chapter, there are at least two strategic considerations that they should keep before them. First, feelings are not something that can be built directly. Feelings result from the persistent conditions that exist in a team's environment. Second, the most persistent and impactful aspect of a team's environment are its values.

Feelings are indirect consequences

The five feelings that are identified in the Model for Superior Team Development and Performance are very much like key indicators for good health. If all five of the feelings of inclusion, commitment, loyalty, pride and trust are strong, then we know that the team is strong and healthy. Everything that goes on in a team affects the feelings of its members and the feelings of its members interact with all the other key elements in the Model for Superior Team Development and Performance to determine the total performance of the team.

It is absurd to imagine that team members can be directed to feel inclusion, or commitment, or loyalty, or anything else. These feelings result from the team being persistent in such things as:

- clarifying its purposes, values, work processes and individual responsibilities
- showing appreciation to its members (individually and collectively) for their value to the team
- ensuring that everyone has the knowledge and skills to perform up to the very highest standards
- extending opportunities for members to have influence over

their jobs, the team and the larger organization (Kinlaw, 1996).

The operational word in strengthening the key feelings is *persistence*. The key feelings are not engendered and maintained by slogans or quick fixes. They are created by clarifying and re-clarifying the team's purposes, priorities, values and responsibilities through every decision that is made and every action taken. The main barrier to strengthening the key feelings is inconsistency.

Imagine a team member told to produce a quality report and then told to do it within absurd time limits. Or consider a team that talks about itself as intending to satisfy its customers 100 per cent of the time and then does not establish a feedback mechanism for maintaining the most intimate kind of contact with its customers.

I know of an architectural firm that is in the process of decline and inevitable demise because it has (on the surface) announced that its intention was to provide its customers with quality designs and drawings, but communicates daily to its drafters and engineers (by its emphasis on meeting schedules) that the real goal is to get as much work out of the door as possible and then worry about fixing it later. People do not produce very well for very long when they work in environments with conflicting values.

The point that I am making is a simple and obvious one. Values must be communicated and reinforced through consistent action and decision-making. One organization with which I have consulted uses the phrase 'walk the talk' to underscore the importance of everyone in the company making its publicized values fully congruent with its actions.

Many organizations and teams claim that their most valuable resource is their people. Today, this is a fairly popular claim. I find this claim a bit difficult to take seriously when I observe that:

● training is offered grudgingly and supervisors nominate people for training, not on the basis of need, but 'who can be spared'

- training is offered only in employee's own time, e.g., Saturdays and after work hours
- people are herded together in spaces that are more appropriate for sheltering cattle than for serious mental activity
- people are treated like children and every minute of their work day is regulated and supervised
- inadequate formal and informal systems for communicating appreciation to people
- how rarely supervisors are evaluated on their performance in developing the knowledge and skills of their people
- executives award bonuses and special privileges to themselves (without, I might say, giving jobholders or shareholders a vote).

The first consideration that teams should keep in mind as they consider strengthening the five key feelings is that these feelings are an indirect result of a multitude of consistent decisions and actions. Slogans and 'motivational' talks will not build inclusion, or commitment, or loyalty. Professions about quality, openness or risk-taking will not build pride or trust. The key feelings that characterize superior teams are built by the whole team 'walking like it talks'.

People in superior teams feel a special way because they work in special environments. To build team-centred organizations, every work unit must have an obvious set of values that provide the grounding for every decision and action.

Values are the main influence
A second consideration for teams is that they recognize that building a clear set of values is the best means they have for strengthening the key feelings. Values, as I have already indicated, are the basis for the kind of consistency that counts. Consistency cannot be established through rules, except in some kind of totally routinized production or work process. In most jobs there are too many unexpected events and problems for each one to be covered by a rule.

Superior teams know, by their experience and their success, that consistently high performance cannot be built on rules, but only on values. The fact is that superior teams have very few rules.

Once a team has established the value, for example, that it intends to have 'enthusiastically positive customers' or that it will 'do everything right the first time' or that 'every worker will be treated with respect', then the day-to-day decisions of people are simple.

In a segment of the old 'Ma Bell' telephone network in the USA, for which I was a consultant for a number of years, I had no doubt that everything that each jobholder did was directed towards the same goal. If you asked any lineman, secretary, crew member or manager the question, 'what is your top priority?' you would get the same answer, 'dial tone'. It was simple for members of that company to know what took preference over everything else.

The key feelings of inclusion, commitment, etc. can only be established, nurtured and strengthened by undeviating consistency in support of a core set of values. Policies and practices, rules and regulations do not build superior teams, they only build conformity.

The values that teams develop should give every team member a clear answer to questions like:

- What do we intend about customer satisfaction?
- How do we expect team members to interact and communicate?
- What are our standards for our services and products?
- What do we intend about continuous improvement?
- What do we expect from each other?

In this chapter I have described the five feelings which make up the third key element in the Model for Superior Team Development and Performance. In the next chapter I will discuss the fourth primary element in the model, leadership.

9 Focusing on leadership

I have now covered three elements in the Model for Superior Team Development and Performance: results, informal processes and feelings. The final primary element in the model is leadership.

The term leadership, as used in the model, carries one specific meaning. It means leadership of teams. The purposes of this chapter are:

- to discuss the special characteristics of the leadership of superior work teams
- to describe the special leadership functions that exist in superior teams.

The discussion of work team leadership that follows is based on information that I have obtained relative to traditional teams that have a team leader or supervisor, as well as on information obtained about self-directed or self-managed teams.

Leadership in a superior work team signifies a set of functions rather than a person. These functions can be performed by one individual or by all the members of a team, i.e., whoever performs a leadership function is, at that moment, leading the team. When I use the term 'leader', I am referring to the *role* of leader and not to a person.

Special characteristics of superior team leadership

Leadership in superior teams is radically different from the way leadership is traditionally understood. In its most general terms, for example, leadership is described as the process of gaining followers. The logic is that to be a leader one must have followers. Leadership requires 'followership'. This kind of logic immediately presents problems for understanding leadership in superior work teams. Leadership in superior teams does not mean creating followers. It means being a team player and creating team players. Leadership in superior teams has the following distinctive characteristics:

- It is always oriented towards the team and teamwork.
- It is always oriented towards both team development and team performance.

Primary orientation towards the team and teamwork

Whoever performs a team leadership function performs that function as a team member and a team player. Team leaders or superior teams approach every task and decision as a potential opportunity for teamwork and as a potential team task. This fundamental orientation towards the team and teamwork has very specific implications for the way team leaders think and act. It means that team leaders focus:

- on team performance more than individual performance
- on creating full involvement of all team members
- on commitment rather than control
- on expanding the team's competency.

Team vs individual performance

Team leaders concentrate on the team and how to encourage maximum team performance more than they concentrate on individuals and how to maximize individual performance. They ensure that the team has team goals, that the work the team does requires the interaction and collaboration of all the team's members, that the team optimizes the competencies of individual members and that the team has measures for the team's performance. They view performance problems as team problems that require team solutions.

In spite of the ever-increasing use of teams and the ever-growing emphasis on teamwork, much modern leadership training is still based on the assumption that the primary unit of performance is the individual. Many leadership training programmes are devoted largely to topics like:

- motivating employees
- delegating
- managing performance
- developing employees
- managing the difficult employee
- interviewing and the like.

Every one of these topics reinforces the notion that the leader's job is to get the most out of individuals. The assumption is that if each individual works harder then the total performance of the group will improve. So education programmes teach leaders:

- how to strengthen the motivation to work of individual employees by using Maslow's hierarchy, Herzberg's job enrichment, behaviour modification or some form of expectancy theory
- how to increase the output of individual employees by delegating more responsibility to each employee
- how to improve individual performance by giving clear direction, feedback and rewards
- how to develop individuals through career planning and individual training plans

- how to manage total individual performance through performance planning and performance appraisals.

One very popular session in most of the leadership training programmes that I have examined in recent years is to have supervisors and managers analyse their personal styles. These sessions use a variety of questionnaires and feedback instruments to assess and rate the styles of the individual manager or supervisor. These styles have an endless variety of classifications, e.g., director, socializer, thinker, intuitor, collaborator, relater and the like. Most of these questionnaires, in one way or another, actually rate how the individual leader interacts with other *individuals*. Again, the bias toward individual behaviour and of leading individuals is apparent. Here, for example, is a set of behaviours that this classification associates with the behavioural style of 'socializer':

- relaxed and warm
- easy to get to know in business
- initiates/accepts physical contact
- patient and co-operative.

Leaders of superior teams do not make less of individuals, relationships with individuals and individual performance than do traditional leaders. Superior team leaders, in fact, have higher expectations for individual performance than do leaders who focus on individuals. Superior team leaders know that individual performance and development are both maximized through teamwork. They also know that the best way to manage individual performance problems is through the power of team membership and team norms.

Traditional work group leaders often waste a great deal of time managing performance problems that fall into two categories: (1) they need never have occurred; and (2) they could have been handled by the team.

In superior teams with well-developed values and norms, many of the problems that worry leaders just do not happen. I have already discussed in Chapter 4, and earlier in this chapter, the core values and clear norms that are so characteristic of superior teams. When there are clear norms about timeliness, co-operation, reliability, integrity and the like, many of the tradition-al performance problems just do not occur. Members of superior teams will typically do everything they can not to break a norm. They value too highly being a member of the team.

Performance problems in superior teams are handled by the team. Everybody enforces and reinforces the values and norms. The way a member of an engineering branch put it was:

The worst feeling I ever had on my team was the time I felt I had let my buddies down. There was a design review meeting that we had with a customer and I had the lead. There was this real obnox-ious character at the meeting who had not attended any of the earlier review meetings and who hadn't bothered to read himself into the project. He kept raising irrelevant questions and pontifi-cating about really stupid issues and I finally lost my cool and let him know what I thought of his contributions. I think I pretty well let him know that he had flawed genes and was playing with a partial deck. Well, my whole team was put on report and we got in deep yoghurt with the customer and also with our division chief. The tough part for me was that the rest of the team let me know that I had thrown months of their hard work out the win-dow. I didn't mind what the chief said to me, but I minded like hell what my team said to me.

When John became our supervisor he made an instant impres-sion. The first day he came on board he called us all together and made a speech. He said that his primary function was to get every-thing that he could for us. He was going to spend his time getting us the training that we wanted and all awards and promotions that we deserved. He said that he was going to spend his time doing everything that he could to provide us with the best pos-sible work environment. He then said that if he was going to spend his time doing all those things, then we would have to do the work and solve most of the problems. John kept his word. And I can tell you this, he was the best supervisor I ever had and we had the best team that I can remember working on.

Because the leaders of superior teams focus on teamwork and team performance, they naturally focus on team rewards more than they do individual awards. In traditional work groups and organizations there are many more individual awards available than there are team awards. The emphasis with them is still on individual performance, individual entrepreneurship and individual competition. Where you find leaders aiming at team performance you will find team awards for quality, productivity, cost savings, innovative ideas, perfect attendance, continuous improvement, cost avoidance and customer satisfaction.

Once teams develop the kind of intense team consciousness that I have found in superior teams, team members themselves begin to consider all their awards to be team awards. In a shop in a Florida engineering firm a mechanic received a $15 000 award for a suggestion for repairing two large air compressors that were slated for salvage and putting the compressors to use in a large heating plant that the company was running. Rather than taking the reward himself, the mechanic directed that it be split among all his team members.

Full involvement of all team members

People who lead superior teams work at keeping every member of the team involved in the team's work and its success. By analysing just how superior teams involve their members, we can produce a set of categories that can serve as a general guide for involving team members. Superior teams consistently involve their members in three general actions, and within these general actions we find three levels of involvement.

Planning

Team leaders find ways to extend opportunities of team members to participate in the various planning processes of the team, e.g., developing team performance goals and measures, planning and organizing work, budget planning, process improvement and planning for change. Team members are involved in planning at three levels:

- *Inputting:* team members provide information, data and suggestions for goals, budgets, work planning, process improvement, planned change and the like.

- *Decision-making:* team members take the decisions about goals, budgets, work planning, process improvement, planned change and the like.
- *Implementing:* team members select and implement the actions and strategies to fulfil goals, budgets, work planning, process improvement, planned change and the like.

Innovating

Superior teams produce new ideas, new products, new technologies and improvements in everything they do. Leaders of superior teams continuously involve team members in the process of innovation at three levels:

- *Inputting:* team members present new ideas, propose new products, propose the use of new technologies and suggest how to improve anything that affects the team's performance.
- *Decision-making:* the whole team is involved in making decisions related to new ideas, new products, new technologies and any way to improve the team's performance.
- *Implementing:* the whole team is involved in acting on new ideas, producing new products, using new technologies and improving the team's performance.

Solving problems

Team leaders view problems as opportunities for a team response to gain team solutions. Problems are viewed as an opportunity to use all the competencies of all the team's members. Team members are involved at the three levels of:

- *Inputting:* every team member is encouraged to identify problems, provide information about the history of a problem, collect data, obtain technical information, diagnose and propose solutions.
- *Decision-making:* the whole team participates in decisions that define a problem and determine how the problem will be addressed.

● *Implementing*: the whole team assumes responsibility for undertaking the actions required to solve a problem.

When we break down the process of involvement as suggested by the foregoing scheme, we produce a set of guidelines that can help teams and team leaders analyse the degree to which all team members are being involved in the work of the team and just how members are being involved. In superior teams, we find that team members are routinely involved at all three levels of inputting, decision-making and implementing.

Commitment vs control

When leaders focus on the team and teamwork they naturally depart from the traditional leadership model of control and move toward a model of leading by commitment. I have already touched on commitment at a number of places earlier and have described commitment as one of the five dominant feelings that are shared by members of superior teams in Chapter 5. In Chapter 6 I described how commitment is one of the natural outcomes of giving people the chance to influence how their work is designed and performed. In that chapter I described how team members behave when they are committed and I also contrasted commitment to control and proposed that leading by commitment was the only leadership strategy that could achieve sustained superior performance. Here, I want to emphasize that gaining commitment of team members is a leadership function.

Building employee commitment – and not building controls – is characteristic of the leaders of superior teams. These leaders know intuitively or from their experience that controls can only produce (at the most) satisfactory performance. The control model is limited for several reasons (Kinlaw, 1989, 1995, 1996a, 1997).

First, it has always been a challenge for leaders of work groups to get people to do what these leaders want. People have always had private goals and priorities that were not fully congruent (all or part of the time) with the leader's or the organization's goals and priorities. And people have always wanted to demonstrate their own competence by doing things 'their own way'. What a number of studies are telling us (as though our own real life experiences were not enough) is that we can expect the demand for job autonomy from people to increase more and more (Boyett and Conn, 1991; Manz and Sims, 1993; Yankelovich and Immerwahr, 1983).

Workers have always valued good pay, a safe and convenient workplace and good fringe benefits. These studies have concluded that jobholders are bringing a new set of psychological demands to their jobs. People are looking for more from their jobs. They want work that is interesting and challenging. And they want more control or autonomy in their jobs.

A second reason for the control model of managing not working very well is that more and more people have more and more discretionary time and energy that they can choose to give or not give to their jobs. Part of this increase has come about because of the kinds of jobs that people now do. We have had an enormous shift in jobs towards the service and professional sector and away from routine jobs in the industrial and manufacturing sector.

I have tested this idea of discretionary effort with thousands of jobholders – from gate guards and refractories mechanics to aerospace engineers and scientists. My findings are consistent. Most people indicate that they could give 15 per cent to 20 per cent more or less effort in their jobs and *nobody would know the difference – especially their supervisors.*

A third limitation to the traditional control model is that most people know more about their specific jobs than anyone else, including their supervisors. There are several reasons that this is true. First, people typically work in jobs that are so complex that they need a great deal of specialization. Also, the technologies of these jobs are always changing.

Here is a personal example to illustrate my point. My small business is dependent upon its computer capability to survive. When I started first using a certain word-processing application software the user's manual was about 1 inch (2.5 cm) thick. The last time I upgraded, the user's manual was about 5 inches (12.5 cm) thick. I could literally devote all of my time to mastering fully that software. It is easy to understand how people are able to make a living just teaching others how to use one or two software applications.

Most managers will usually admit that their secretaries know more about their business than they (the managers) do. Now, the gap between what secretaries know and managers do not is becoming wider and wider. Consider the equipment available to most secretaries. They have PCs and modems. They manage and use networks, electronic mail, corporate calendars, fax machines and databases. The changes in the knowledge bases of secretaries are certain to increase the dependence of managers and the autonomy of secretaries.

A fourth limitation to the control model results from work environments that are so filled with problems, so unstable – if not chaotic – that leaders often cannot predict what it is that needs to be done in order to achieve the results that they are after.

The main value that jobholders have for their companies is that they solve problems, they take care of the unexpected and they take advantage of unanticipated opportunities. People are often most valuable because they do what no one could have predicted beforehand needed doing.

A fifth limitation to the control model is that controls will not take full advantage of the human resources that are available in a work group. Leaders who operate from the control model will consistently underutilize people and make poor use of their potential. The reason for this is that they will fail to look for ways to extend the influence of people and thereby give them more opportunities to demonstrate their competencies.

In this section I have been discussing one of the characteristics that distinguishes superior team leadership from traditional leadership, i.e. that its primary orientation to performing every aspect of work is towards the team and teamwork. This fundamental orientation towards the team and teamwork has very specific implications for the way team leaders think and act. I have proposed that team leaders concentrate:

- on team performance more than individual performance
- on creating full involvement of all team members
- on commitment rather than control

- on expanding the team's competency.

I have now covered the first three of these foci and turn now to the final one.

Expanding the team's competency

In Chapter 6 I identified the first result produced by superior teams as, the maximum use of the team's mental resources. I described in that chapter just how superior teams encourage and support the development of individual and team competencies. I also identified three leadership behaviours which lead to the growth of individuals and team competency. These were:

1 Expecting people to be competent.
2 Giving people the opportunity to show that they are competent.
3 Giving people the support required to become more competent.

There is no need to repeat the discussion about competency here and the responsibilities that team leaders have for developing such competency. One main strategy for building competencies is by coaching. Coaching is a significant function of team leadership and I cover this topic later in this chapter.

Orientation towards team development and team performance

Team leadership is always oriented towards the team and teamwork. It has a second main characteristic. Superior team leaders recognize that team development and team performance are inseparable. They know that the more fully developed the team becomes the better it will perform.

One of the most consistent and glaring errors that work team leaders commit is that they stay so involved with getting the job done that they fail to build the team's potential for doing the job.

Team development is the primary means for building the team's potential.

My experience with work group leaders over and over again is that somehow leaders imagine that the development of their work units into fully functioning teams will take place as a natural result of people being involved together in the same unit. My experience also indicates that the most frequent underlying cause of problems in work groups is that the group has never developed into a team.

I recently conducted a survey of work groups in a design engineering group of some 350 people. Twenty-six work groups were involved. Recently I began to follow up with a sample set of work groups to determine how the groups had used the data, what changes they had targeted and exactly how they planned to reach their targets. Here are two of my findings:

1   The groups that scored high on the portions of the survey that measured team development have made better use of the survey to improve their performance than the groups that scored low on team development.
2   The groups that used teamwork to analyse their group's data have developed far more initiatives to improve their performance than those groups in which the group's supervisor assumed responsibility for the data.

Teamwork is the key to both team development and superior performance. Superior team leaders understand that teams do not perform one minute and then develop themselves into teams the next.

The Model for Superior Team Development and Performance provides a number of alternative ways to see clearly just how team development and team performance are associated. Take for example the key results of:

● maximum use of team's human resources
● highly satisfied customers
● superior outputs against all odds
● continuous improvement.

Only fully developed teams can attain these results. I have observed over and over again just how critical the connection is between team development and team results. Here are a few examples that I have selected from a very large file.

One group had been formed for about a year. The people were assigned to the group without consultation with the prospective supervisor. The group was given two older engineers who were near retirement, six recently graduated engineers and a secretary who had very poor interpersonal skills and who had previously been on probation for poor performance. The group supervisor responded to one interpersonal and performance crisis after the other. Each time he went on leave he returned to face one or more catastrophes. Periodically he was hauled on the mat by his boss and told to straighten his group out. He never made the connection between team development and performance and so he never considered ways to involve the team in solving its own problems, i.e., through teamwork. My last information indicated that the group had not improved and that senior management was considering ways to reorganize it out of existence.

Another group was described to me recently that was located in the headquarters of a large organization. The group was in charge of a variety of training and personnel functions. The group's senior manager was replaced and the new manager decided to hold a team-building retreat. He also decided that, because the team was made up largely of experienced human resources professionals, the group would not need a trained facilitator. His trained group of professionals acquiesced in his decision. Without a trained facilitator the retreat degenerated into disorder. No resolution of all the problems that were identified at the retreat has ever been attempted and the many interpersonal issues have never been resolved. The group's performance has been acknowledged by most of its members as marginal and yet no one has made any serious attempt to connect the group's performance to its level of team development.

Superior team leaders know that the possibility of superior performance only exists where there is superior team development. These leaders know that they must focus on developing the team in order to achieve superior performance.

Superior leadership functions

There are at least three functions which are associated with the leaders of superior work teams. These are:

- initiator
- model
- coach.

Initiator

Superior leaders initiate the various actions and processes for building their work units into superior teams. The basic guideline for initiating team development is to make teamwork the norm for all actions. The way to initiate team development is to involve the team at the very outset in the process.

The Model for Superior Team Development and Performance provides a template for team development actions. One characteristic of the model that I have emphasized at various points in this book is that the model views team development and performance to be, first, the result of a conscious decision by a work group to be a superior team. The decision to be a superior team is more important than how well the group's tasks lend themselves to team performance, i.e., require integration among the members. The entire model and the information that I have provided thus far provide any work group with quite an array of options for developing itself as a team and improving its performance. Nothing in the model has any practical utility unless the model is used by a work unit that is interested in becoming a superior team. The model reflects what superior teams look like and denotes what any team, group or unit can do to become a superior team.

Initiating team development is largely a process of setting goals. Goal-setting has been shown to be the most consistently reliable strategy for influencing performance. Goal-setting has an impact on the direction of a team's effort, on the strength of a team's effort and on the duration or persistence of a team's effort (Locke et al., 1981). It is also the case that the more specific the goals, the more likely it is that teams will develop effective strategies for achieving them.

The initiator function of a team leader largely means that the leader helps bring the work group to make the following conscious decisions:

1 Reaffirm in a clear, unambiguous way the intention to become or continue to improve as a superior team.
2 Set aside quality time to develop strategies and identify opportunities for significant improvement as a team.
3 Determine what near and long-term changes should be planned to ensure that the team is structured to continue to develop and function as a superior team.
4 Consider the long-term future of the team and the kinds of knowledge and skills that the team must have to continue as a superior team.

The first function that a team leader occupies is initiator. The second function is model.

Model

The team leader models the kind of performance and behaviour that serve to develop the team. In the simplest terms this means that the team leader models what is expected of team members.

What I have already identified in the Model for Superior Team Development and Performance as the fundamental characteristics of a superior team are the very characteristics that I have found embodied in superior team leaders. Team leaders model team membership in two ways. First they model it in the way they conduct their own business and perform their own tasks. Second, they model team membership in the way they interact with their colleagues.

Results

Take, for instance, the three sub-elements in the key element, results. Team leaders model the results of making maximum use of human resources, achieving superior outputs against all odds and showing continuous improvement. They are models, first, by embodying the processes in themselves. They are also models in the way that they interact with the team.

Take, for example, making maximum use of a team's human resources. They are, first, models of this result in the way they are committed to using their own competencies and in developing new competencies. They are perceived as persons who are hard-working, curious, continuously learning and who actively seek new opportunities to apply their competencies. They accept personal challenges and are seen as persons who are easily taught by others.

Team leaders also model what it means to make the maximum use of human resources in their interactions with others. They delegate easily and avoid micromanagement. They fully support the training of all team members and aggressively go after resources to support training. They help other team members cope positively with disappointments and failures. They ensure that other team members are involved in tasks that they feel are challenging and interesting.

What I have observed about the process of making maximum use of a team's human resources also pertains to the other results of superior outputs against all odds and continuous improvement. Superior leaders model these results in what they personally achieve in the way they take action to ensure that the team achieves these results.

Processes

Team leaders model the processes in the Model for Superior Team Development and Performance. They model communicating and contacting, responding and adapting, influencing and improving, appreciating and celebrating. First, they model these processes in their own behaviours. Second, they model these behaviours in the actions they take to ensure that the processes are alive and well throughout the whole team.

Take, for example, communicating and contacting. Superior team leaders model this process in their own behaviour by making frequent informal contact with other team members. They model good listening and problem-solving skills. They make it easy for others to be frank and open in the way they communicate. They are easily available.

They also model the process in the actions they take to ensure that other team members communicate and stay in contact. They work at simplifying paperwork because they know that paper is a barrier to personal contact. They hold regular team meetings.

What I have observed about communicating and contacting is true of the other three processes. Superior leaders model these processes in their own behaviour and in the actions they take to ensure that the processes are functioning throughout the team.

Feelings

Superior team leaders know what it feels like to be a member of a superior team. They model the behaviours that support the development of these feelings in themselves and in others. They nurture the sense of inclusion by a variety of actions. Superior team leaders ensure that:

- they have balanced contact with all team members
- team members get the information that affects their job and their life in the organization
- the right team members attend the right meetings
- team members are involved in decisions that are made that affect them
- everyone's ideas are treated with respect
- all team members have a fair chance at challenging work
- appreciation is communicated to team members for their performance and value to the team
- radical concern is shown for each team member's well-being
- people have the chance to demonstrate their full competence
- there are frequent opportunities for team members to participate together in a variety of social events.

I have now briefly discussed the first two functions that superior team leaders frequently occupy: initiator and model. The third function is coach.

Coach

Coaching has emerged as a commonly accepted function for team leaders (Katzenbach and Smith, 1993; Wellins, Byham and Dixon, 1994; Zenger, et al., 1994). From my study of superior work teams it is clearly apparent that coaching is a necessary and pervasive activity among team members.

I have treated the subject of coaching in detail in an earlier book (Kinlaw, 1997) and I will not repeat that information here. What I will do is describe briefly what coaching is and outline its four main functions. The reader who would like to have a full treatment of coaching is encouraged to consult my *Coaching: Winning Strategies for Individuals and Teams*, published by Gower .

Coaching is a disciplined personal interaction with one or more persons which produces winning results for individuals, teams and organizations by focusing and refocusing them on performance goals and facilitating their achievement of these goals.

Coaching includes a variety of interactions the purpose of which is to improve performance. These interactions can be brief or extended. Coaching interactions that tend to be brief are interactions with the purpose:

- to give feedback
- to encourage or
- to reward.

Coaching interactions which tend to be formal and extended have the purpose:

- to instruct
- to solve problems
- to challenge or
- to improve performance.

The successful coaching of teams needs the same interpersonal skills that are required for coaching individuals. In many instances, of course, team members may be coached as individuals. Paramount among such skills are those which:

- communicate attention;
- develop information;
- convey support and confidence.

Coaching a whole team, however, needs some additional skills:

1   special knowledge and skills for helping a team manage its meetings
2   the team coach must be able to help a team use special team problem-solving tools.

I have now described in some detail the dominant characteristics of superior teams. A review of the Model for Superior Team Development and Performance in Chapter 5 will show that, at the centre of the four major characteristics of superior teams are *tools*. In the Appendix you will find described a set of proven tools for helping you develop your superior team.

Conclusion

This book has been about superior teams. My underlying assumption has been that sustained, superior performance is only possible through superior teams. The companies that will continue to outperform their competitors will be those which use team formation and teamwork as their primary organizing principles. Understanding the process of team formation and development will become more and more a leadership priority, and those leaders who will become most indispensable are those who have the fullest understanding of the team-centred organization and the fullest commitment to such an organization.

It is becoming less common that leaders in organizations do not understand the value of teams and teamwork. During the past half-dozen years, we can observe the passing of most of the resistances that managers and supervisors once felt about the formation and use of teams. Leaders rarely need to be convinced about the value of teams and teamwork. What most of them want is help.

I have offered such help in this book by providing specific solutions to the most common questions that people have about teams. I have:

- described a foundation for building a team-centred organization by demonstrating how teams differ from groups, and superior teams differ from teams
- shown how team development can be a deliberate, planned activity and avoid many of the problems often associated with team development
- described the many opportunities that exist for forming and using teams
- described the kind of organizational support that must exist for superior teams to develop and grow, and the kinds of strategies that can be used to build a team-centred organization.
- defined a set of proven steps for forming and developing teams
- discussed in detail the special characteristics that are typical of superior teams.

A large portion of this book has been devoted to describing and explaining the Model for Superior Team Development and Performance. As I have covered the model, I have several times referred to certain tools that have great utility for developing superior teams. You will find a description of these tools in the Appendix.

I can think of no better way to end a book on superior teams than to describe one of the superior teams that I met during my study. The team was an air compressor shop of a US engineering firm. The shop had eight members and all members except the supervisor were members of a union. The age of the shop's members ran from late twenties to early fifties.

This team received so many cash awards through the company's continuous improvement programme that some of the rules for rewards had to be rewritten. In a two-year period, the team shared bonuses of $35 000.

The members that I had a chance to interview in some depth described just how wonderful it was to go to work. They talked about actually missing the job and their team members when they were not on their jobs. They talked about the almost unbelievable experience of never having a 'bad day' at work. Far-fetched as it may sound, I concluded from my interviews and observations that each of the members of this team were always 'up', always happy in their jobs, and somewhat outrageous in the way they thought about themselves. Over and over again, one after the other of them said to me that they 'had the best team of its kind', that they were 'the best team in the company', and 'they wouldn't trade jobs with anybody'. These remarks were made by the younger members of the team as well as the older ones.

In this team, there were no distinctions made among members because of age. The older men went out of their way to tell me just how bright and valuable were the younger members. The younger members volunteered to tell me how much they continued to learn from the older members.

The team's admiration of their supervisor was so positive that I felt self-conscious at times listening to what the members said. 'He is the best there is.' 'I have worked with him for five years and we have never once even had a cross word.' 'There ain't nobody around who can do what he can do.' One member put his experience on the team in perspective by describing his previous experience in two companies prior to his present job:

This is the first time that I have had a chance to think. Mr——, our top man, came down when this team was put together and told us he expected us to think and that we were getting paid to think. He told us that if we could do anything better or make any kinds of improvements then do it. Where I used to work, we were treated like kids. We could never start a job unless our supervisor told us to. And every single detail was laid out. You had to go ahead and do a job, even when you knew it was being done wrong and that you would have to come back and do it over. If you wanted your butt kicked, just do anything at all that you weren't told to do. What ticked me off was that everything was so political. You got the jobs to do because of how well the supervisor liked you. And overtime was passed out the same way. I hated my job. I used to feel physically sick a lot. But now, it's like the difference between night and day. This is the greatest company in the world and I work with the greatest bunch of guys in the world. Now I've got only one problem and that is dealing with the people who are just plain jealous of us and how good we've got it.

One senior manager confided to me that his biggest problem was trying to enforce a few controls just to keep this team from creating too many problems with other people who had turfs to protect:

This is a union shop remember. These guys have a habit of putting their other union buddies on notice. They will tell the painters and maintenance people for instance, 'we want this or that painted by such and such a date and if you don't do it, we will do it ourselves'. They do so much more than most other teams because they just won't let the formal system stop them. And they are able to get away with it most of the time because they have done so many favours for so many people that everyone owes them and they just keep calling in their chips.

Superior teams are the single comprehensive answer to improved performance. They are a proven strategy for ensuring quality in services and products. They certainly provide the solution to gaining a competitive edge in the market-place. As it turns out, however, superior teams achieve much more. They provide people with the best chance to be fulfilled and happy in their work.

Appendix: tools for developing superior teams

The tools in this Appendix can be used to serve the following developmental purposes:

1   As analytical and assessment tools to identify team strengths and opportunities.
2   To educate team members about key issues in team development.
3   To devise very specific team development actions.
4   To build baseline data for tracking team development and performance over time.
5   To develop common symbols and a common team vocabulary about development and performance.
6   To communicate team development actions and successes to outsiders.

Included in this Appendix are the following tools for developing superior teams:

● using the Model for Superior Team Development and Performance

- using the Superior Team Development Inventory
- using the General Systems Model of Team Performance.

Using the Model for Superior Team Development and Performance

The most comprehensive tool for developing superior teams is the Model for Superior Team Development and Performance itself (Figure 5.1). The model provides the conceptual basis for understanding superior teams and it provides an outline for planning superior team development and performance. In Chapter 4, Figure 4.2, I identified as a main step in superior team development, selecting and using the Model for Superior Team Development and Performance.

The first step in using the model is to understand it. Here is a team approach to understanding the model:

1   The team reviews the model and each of the four primary characteristics: results, informal processes, feelings, and leadership. A recommended progression to follow is:
    - one team member presents an overview of the model
    - team members discuss the model and develop a common understanding of what it describes.
2   The team reviews each of the characteristics and its elements in depth. A recommended progression to follow is:
    - one team member presents an overview of the first characteristic, results and its elements
    - team members discuss the characteristic and its elements and identify how they might begin to strengthen each element within the team.

The model, once understood, can be used in a number of ways to guide the team towards continuous improvement. For example, it can become the basis for reviewing the team's initial norms. One space engineering company, for example, decided to incorporate the five feelings of inclusion, commitment, loyalty, pride, and trust into a set of norms that were used to govern the performance of all the company's teams. It can also become a tool for identifying a variety of improvement opportunities. Each element of each characteristic can become the basis for discussing the team's performance and for identifying issues and opportunities. Take the first characteristic of results. Just by reviewing the meaning of this characteristic and its elements, teams will ask how well they are producing outputs fit to use 100 per cent of the time, how well they are satisfying their internal and external customers, and what they are doing to ensure the maximum development and use of the team's human resources.

Using the superior team development inventory (STDI)

The information provided in this section applies to all of the four parts of the STDI.

Description of the STDI

The STDI has four parts. Each part corresponds to one of the four characteristics identified in the Model for Superior Team Development and Performance. Each characteristic has several elements. The four parts and their elements are shown below. The number in parentheses, following each of the characteristics denotes the number of items in that part of the STDI. The numbers in parentheses following each of the elements, refers to the items in the STDI which measure that element.

Part 1: Focusing on superior results (30 items)

- Maximum use of human resources (items 1–10)
- Customer satisfaction and superior outputs (items 11–20)
- Continuous improvement (items 21–30).

Part 2: Focusing on informal processes (40 items)

- Communicating and contacting (items 1–10)
- Responding and adapting (items 11–20)

- Influencing and improving (items 21–30)
- Appreciating and celebrating (items 31–40).

Part 3: Focusing on feelings (50 items)

- Inclusion (items 1–10)
- Commitment (11–20)
- Loyalty (21–30)
- Pride (31–40)
- Trust (41-50).

Part 4: Focusing on leadership (30 items)

- Initiator (1–10)
- Model (11–20)
- Coach (21–30).

Scoring the STDI

All four parts of the STDI are scored the same way. Each part of the STDI measures one of the four general characteristics of superior teams identified in the Model for Superior Team Development and Performance. Each characteristic has a set of elements, e.g., Part 3 has five elements: inclusion, commitment, loyalty, pride and trust. Each of the elements has ten items on the STDI. Team summary ratings are computed for each element within each characteristic and each item within each element. Here is the process for scoring and summarizing the STDI:

1 Each team member completes all of the items for one part of the STDI by recording ratings on the answer sheet provided. The STDI summary rating sheets found below can be used for ease in summarizing the team's responses. Directions for summarizing data follow.
2 Compute the total frequency of responses for each item, i.e. the number of 1s, 2s, 3s, 4s and 5s.
3 Compute the team's average rating for each item. For each of the five possible ratings (1 through 5), multiply the number of times it was used by the value of the rating. Then divide the

sum of these five products by the number of members and record the average. For example, if six participants gave a rating of 5 (6 × 5 = 30), five gave ratings of 4 (5 × 4 = 20), four gave ratings of 3 (4 × 3 = 12), three gave ratings of 2 (3 × 2 = 6), and 2 gave ratings of 1 (2 × 1 = 2), the arithmetic average would be: (30+20+12+6+2)/20 = 3.50.

4   Compute the team's overall frequency of responses for each element by adding the number of 1s, 2s, 3s, 4s, and 5s.
5   Compute the team's overall average for each element by dividing the sum of the average rating for each of the items by the number of items.
6   Compute the percentage of responses that are 4s and 5s for each element by dividing the sum of all 4s and 5s by the total number of responses (usually the number of participants multiplied by 10).
7   Compute the percentage of responses that are 1s, 2s and 3s for each element by dividing the sum of all 1s, 2s, and 3s by the total number of responses (usually the number of participants multiplied by 10).

Interpretation of STDI

The purpose in using the STDI is to help team members identify the strengths of their teams, to identify improvement opportunities and to plan specific improvement initiatives. We can identify strengths and opportunities in several ways, using the STDI:

- First, teams should look at their ratings for each element within a characteristic. For example, within Part 3: Focus on feelings, teams should look at the summary ratings for each of the elements: inclusion, commitment, loyalty, pride and trust.
- Second, teams should examine each item within each element to look for opportunities for improvement. For example, within the element, Inclusion, of Part 3: Focus on feelings, there are 10 items. Each item must be looked at to determine if the rating on that item suggests an opportunity for improvement.

Strengths

1 Strengths are indicated in the STDI if any of the elements within any of the four characteristics has a summary rating of 3.85 or higher *and* if the summary frequency of 4 and 5 ratings for the element is at least 65 per cent of the total number of ratings. If, for example, Maximum use of human resources, within Part 1: Focusing on results received a summary rating of 3.85 or higher *and* if the summary frequency of 4 and 5 ratings was at least 65 per cent, then Maximum use of human resources would be a major strength for the team.
2 Second-order strengths are identified in the STDI if any of the items within an element has a rating of 3.85 or higher and 65 per cent of the ratings are 4 or 5.

Opportunities

1 Opportunities are indicated in the STDI if any of the elements within any of the four characteristics has a summary rating less than 3.85 or if the summary frequency of 4 and 5 ratings for the element is less than 65 per cent of the total number of ratings. If, for example, Maximum use of human resources, within Part 1: Focusing on results received a summary rating of less than 3.85 or if the summary frequency of 4 and 5 ratings was at less than 65 per cent, then Maximum use of human resources would still be a major opportunity for the team.
2 Second-order opportunities are identified in the STDI if any of the items within an element has a rating of less than 3.85 or 65 per cent of the ratings are not 4 or 5.

Example
Below you will find an example of a rating for the element Loyalty within the characteristic, feelings, measured by Part 3: Focus on feelings of the STDI. From the information contained in this example we can make the following conclusions for Loyalty about the team being rated:

1 Average for the element is less than 3.85.
2 Percentage of 4 and 5 ratings is less than 65 per cent.
3 Ten of ten items have averages of less than 3.85.
4 The element and all its items are opportunities for improvement.

LOYALTY	RATING FREQUENCY					
ITEM	**1**	**2**	**3**	**4**	**5**	**AVG**
21	2	3	4	5	6	3.50
22	6	5	4	3	2	2.50
23	3	4	5	6	2	3.00
24	5	6	2	3	4	2.75
25	2	3	3	5	7	3.60
26	5	6	2	3	4	2.75
27	4	3	2	6	5	3.25
28	2	3	3	5	7	3.60
29	3	4	5	6	2	3.00
30	5	6	2	3	4	2.75
FREQUENCY	37	43	32	45	43	
Participants: 20	Percentage of 1,2,3		56%	Percentage of 4,5	44%	OVERALL AVG 3.07

Steps to interpret STDI

Step 1 Determine if the element is a strength or an improvement opportunity. If the element is a *strength*, go to step 2; if the element is an *improvement opportunity*, go to step 3.

Step 2 If the element is a *strength*, proceed as follows:

2.1: Have each member relate why he/she thinks this element may be as a strength and give specific personal experiences that may support the group's positive rating. Record these experiences so that you can refer to them later on.

2.2: Discuss each of the ten items on the STDI that are included with the element as a guide and through a general discussion develop a list of actions that your team is now doing to ensure that this element is a strength. Record these actions so that you can refer to them later on.

Step 3 If the element is an *improvement opportunity*, proceed as follows:

3.1: Have each member relate why he/she thinks this element may be an improvement opportunity and give specific personal experiences that may support the team's negative rating. Record these experiences so that you can refer to them later on.

3.2: Review each of the ten items in the STDI for the element and discuss in detail all items that have an average of less than 3.85 or for which the frequency of 4s and 5s is less than 65 per cent. Is the negative rating or low frequency of 4s and 5s important to the group? What might be done to strengthen the item? Record the information developed in this step so that you can refer to them later on.

Step 4 Review the information developed from the previous step (2 or 3). Are there any improvement targets that your team should address? If so, record these targets for later reference when your team designs its improvement projects.

Step 5 In the previous step you identified some possible improvement targets. List all of these targets on chart paper so the whole team can see them and refer to them. Review the list and determine if there are other targets that should be listed. Select the targets that you want to turn into improvement projects.

KINLAW ASSOCIATES
255 College Cross, No. 77
Norfolk, Virginia 23510

Author: Dennis C. Kinlaw, Ed.D.

SUPERIOR TEAM DEVELOPMENT INVENTORY: PART 1

FOCUSING ON SUPERIOR RESULTS

Directions

n completing the **Superior Team Development Inventory: Part 1** you must be con-
istent about the 'team' you are rating. The team you are rating consists of you and all
he other people who are involved with you as a team in the **Superior Team
Development System**.

Follow the steps below and complete this part of the **Inventory**.

1. Indicate the company or organization to which you belong, e.g., Aerospace
echnical Services, Last National Bank, Speedy Supply, etc. and the date on which
ou are completing this part of the **Superior Team Development Inventory (STDI)**.

Company/Organization _____ Date _____

2. Name the team on which you are completing the STDI.

eam _____

3. Each item in the STDI presents a characteristic that may describe your team to
ome degree or which may not describe your team at all. Indicate the degree to which
ou believe the item accurately describes your own team by circling the appropriate
umber on the scale (5 to 1) that appears with each item. '5' indicates that you com-
letely agree. '1' indicates that you do not agree at all.

4. Complete **every** item.

5. Follow any special instructions that your team may have established for turn-
g in and scoring your completed STDI: Part 1.

CONTINUE TO NEXT PAGE

	COMPLETELY AGREE				DO NOT AGREE AT ALL

IN THE TEAM I AM RATING:

1. The norm is for every member to be learning something new all the time.

| 5 | 4 | 3 | 2 | 1 |

2. We are all quick to share anything we know with each other – if we think it will help the other person do his/her job.

| 5 | 4 | 3 | 2 | 1 |

3. We make maximum use of each other's competencies.

| 5 | 4 | 3 | 2 | 1 |

4. We make it easy for our members to attend training and education programmes.

| 5 | 4 | 3 | 2 | 1 |

5. We involve the whole team in determining what competencies each member of the team needs.

| 5 | 4 | 3 | 2 | 1 |

6. We make a special point of encouraging new members to apply their competencies.

| 5 | 4 | 3 | 2 | 1 |

7. We encourage members to take on jobs that require them to learn something new.

| 5 | 4 | 3 | 2 | 1 |

8. To be a leader you must be viewed as a good teacher.

| 5 | 4 | 3 | 2 | 1 |

9. We ensure that each of us is cross-trained for more than one job.

| 5 | 4 | 3 | 2 | 1 |

	COMPLETELY AGREE				DO NOT AGREE AT ALL

IN THE TEAM I AM RATING:

10.   We regularly bring in outside experts to keep us aware of new developments related to our jobs.

5	4	3	2	1

11.   We always deliver what we say we will.

5	4	3	2	1

12.   We never sacrifice the quality of our services and products for any reason.

5	4	3	2	1

13.   We always find ways to work around problems that could block successfully completing our job.

5	4	3	2	1

14.   We continuously measure the quality of our services and products.

5	4	3	2	1

15.   We always know what work is most important to our team at any given time.

5	4	3	2	1

16.   We always expect that our services and products will be the best.

5	4	3	2	1

17. We typically anticipate problems that might have an adverse impact on our work.

5	4	3	2	1

18.   We consciously build relationships with other people who might contribute to our team's performance.

5	4	3	2	1

	COMPLETELY AGREE				DO NOT AGREE AT ALL

IN THE TEAM I AM RATING:

19. Our team's goals typically take precedence over the goals of individual members.

    5   4   3   2   1

20. It is easy for anyone to question the value of any aspect of our work.

    5   4   3   2   1

21. New ideas are taken seriously.

    5   4   3   2   1

22. We always have improvement targets that we are working on.

    5   4   3   2   1

23. We have regular team meetings that are totally devoted to working on improvement opportunities.

    5   4   3   2   1

24. We regularly analyse the processes by which we do our work.

    5   4   3   2   1

25. We are working with all of our internal customers to ensure their complete satisfaction with our services and products.

    5   4   3   2   1

26. We are working with all of our external customers to ensure their complete satisfaction with our services and products.

    5   4   3   2   1

27. We are working with all of our internal suppliers to improve the services and products of theirs that we use.

    5   4   3   2   1

	COMPLETELY AGREE				DO NOT AGREE AT ALL

N THE TEAM I AM RATING:

8. We are working with all of ur external suppliers to improve he services and products of theirs hat we use.	5	4	3	2	1
9. We consider continuous mprovement to be part of veryone's routine job.	5	4	3	2	1
0. We have a documented record f improvements we have made in he quality of our team's erformance.	5	4	3	2	1

END

KINLAW ASSOCIATES
255 College Cross, No. 77
Norfolk, Virginia 23510

Author: Dennis C. Kinlaw, Ed.D.

SUPERIOR TEAM DEVELOPMENT INVENTORY: PART 2

FOCUSING ON INFORMAL PROCESSES

Directions

In completing the **Superior Team Development Inventory: Part 2** you must be consistent about the 'team' you are rating. The team you are rating consists of you and all the other people who are involved with you as a team in the **Superior Team Development System**.

Follow the steps below and complete this part of the **Inventory**.

1.   Indicate the company or organization to which you belong, e.g., Aerospace Technical Services, Last National Bank, Speedy Supply, etc. and the date on which you are completing this part of the **Superior Team Development Inventory (STDI)**.

Company/Organization _____ Date _____

2.   Name the team on which you are completing the STDI.

Team _____

3.   Each item in the STDI presents a characteristic that may describe your team to some degree or which may not describe your team at all. Indicate the degree to which you believe the item accurately describes your own team by circling the appropriate number on the scale (5 to 1) that appears with each item. '5' indicates that you completely agree. '1' indicates that you do not agree at all.

4.   Complete **every** item.

5.   Follow any special instructions that your team may have established for turning in and scoring your completed STDI: Part 2.

CONTINUE TO NEXT PAGE

	COMPLETELY AGREE				DO NOT AGREE AT ALL

IN THE TEAM I AM RATING:

1. It is easy to get in touch with any other team member when you need to.	5	4	3	2	1
2. When you talk to another team member you have the sense of being fully respected.	5	4	3	2	1
3. Our supervisors and other team leaders are in touch with the team's other members at least once a day.	5	4	3	2	1
4. We make sure that no one is 'surprised' by information that he/she should have had.	5	4	3	2	1
5. Members listen well to each other.	5	4	3	2	1
6. Members are easy to talk to.	5	4	3	2	1
7. We have regular team meetings to share information with each other.	5	4	3	2	1
8. When one team member needs to solve a problem it is easy to get an informal meeting going with other members who might help.	5	4	3	2	1

	COMPLETELY AGREE				DO NOT AGREE AT ALL

IN THE TEAM I AM RATING:

9.   We make sure our members get the training they need in interpersonal communication.

5	4	3	2	1

10.   We solve conflicts among us immediately that might interfere with our communication.

5	4	3	2	1

11.   We get prompt decisions from our supervisors and other team leaders when we need them.

5	4	3	2	1

12.   When you ask another team member for help you get it promptly.

5	4	3	2	1

13.   Members are quick to offer you help even before you ask for it.

5	4	3	2	1

14.   We are able quickly to change directions and reorder our priorities when we have to.

5	4	3	2	1

15.   When you ask someone for help you are never made to feel like you are imposing on the other person's time.

5	4	3	2	1

16.   It is a norm in our team that the other person's job is as important as your own.

5	4	3	2	1

	COMPLETELY AGREE				DO NOT AGREE AT ALL

IN THE TEAM I AM RATING:

17. We value co-operation and not competition.	5	4	3	2	1
18. We make a special effort to show our appreciation to members who have gone out of their way to help their fellow team members.	5	4	3	2	1
19. If you have some personal problem that comes up it is easy to get the special consideration you might need to solve it.	5	4	3	2	1
20. Members always focus on making the team look good rather than making themselves look good.	5	4	3	2	1
21. It is easy for each member to improve how his/her job is done.	5	4	3	2	1
22. It is easy for each team member to improve how the team performs.	5	4	3	2	1
23. We encourage every-one to make improvement suggestions of every kind.	5	4	3	2	1
24. The people who are closest to a problem always get the first shot at fixing it.	5	4	3	2	1

	COMPLETELY AGREE				**DO NOT AGREE AT ALL**

IN THE TEAM I AM RATING:

25.   We expect members to give feedback to each other to improve the way we do our jobs.

| | 5 | 4 | 3 | 2 | 1 |

26.   We make sure our members are involved when plans are made that might affect them.

| | 5 | 4 | 3 | 2 | 1 |

27.   We have a lot of freedom to test our own ideas.

| | 5 | 4 | 3 | 2 | 1 |

28.   It is easy for members to speak their minds when they don't agree with something.

| | 5 | 4 | 3 | 2 | 1 |

29.   Members have more influence based on what they know than on what position they have.

| | 5 | 4 | 3 | 2 | 1 |

30.   We use the competencies of all our team members to ensure that we make the best possible decisions.

| | 5 | 4 | 3 | 2 | 1 |

31.   We make the maximum use of the formal awards in our organization to reward our members.

| | 5 | 4 | 3 | 2 | 1 |

32.   We frequently show our appreciation to each other in informal ways.

| | 5 | 4 | 3 | 2 | 1 |

	COMPLETELY AGREE				DO NOT AGREE AT ALL

IN THE TEAM I AM RATING:

33. We ensure that all our team members have an equal chance for visibility with senior management.

5	4	3	2	1

34. We make sure that each person knows how he/she contributes to the team's success.

5	4	3	2	1

35. Members who perform the less glamorous jobs are appreciated as much as those who perform the more glamorous jobs.

5	4	3	2	1

36. Each person has a strong sense of being needed by the whole team.

5	4	3	2	1

37. No one ever takes the credit for another team member's achievement.

5	4	3	2	1

38. We ensure that each member has a chance to do interesting and challenging work.

5	4	3	2	1

39. We regularly celebrate our whole team's achievements.

5	4	3	2	1

40. We don't blame our members for problems – we focus on fixing the problems.

5	4	3	2	1

END

KINLAW ASSOCIATES
255 College Cross, No. 77
Norfolk, Virginia 23510

Author: Dennis C. Kinlaw, Ed.D.

SUPERIOR TEAM DEVELOPMENT INVENTORY: PART 3

FOCUSING ON FEELINGS

Directions

In completing the **Superior Team Development Inventory: Part 3** you must be consistent about the 'team' you are rating. The team you are rating consists of you and all the other people who are involved with you as a team in the **Superior Team Development System**.

Follow the steps below and complete this part of the **Inventory**.

1.　Indicate the company or organization to which you belong, e.g., Aerospace Technical Services, Last National Bank, Speedy Supply, etc. and the date on which you are completing this part of the **Superior Team Development Inventory (STDI)**.

Company/Organization _____ Date _____

2.　Name the team on which you are completing the STDI.

Team _____

3.　Each item in the STDI presents a characteristic that may describe your team to some degree or which may not describe your team at all. Indicate the degree to which you believe the item accurately describes your own team by circling the appropriate number on the scale (5 to 1) that appears with each item. '5' indicates that you completely agree. '1' indicates that you do not agree at all.

4.　Complete **every** item.

5.　Follow any special instructions that your team may have established for turning in and scoring your completed STDI: Part 3.

CONTINUE TO NEXT PAGE

	COMPLETELY AGREE				DO NOT AGREE AT ALL

IN THE TEAM I AM RATING:

1. My input on any aspect of our team's work is taken seriously.	5	4	3	2	1
2. I am taken into account on all changes that affect me.	5	4	3	2	1
3. There are no cliques that exclude me.	5	4	3	2	1
4. I am fully recognized for my contributions to the team's performance.	5	4	3	2	1
5. I am always treated with respect by other members.	5	4	3	2	1
6. I make an important contribution to the team's goals.	5	4	3	2	1
7. Nothing on our team is done in secret and I can get as much information as I want.	5	4	3	2	1
8. I have as many privileges as anyone else.	5	4	3	2	1
9. People go out of their way to help me get the information needed to do my best work.	5	4	3	2	1
10. I am included in the team's social events.	5	4	3	2	1

	COMPLETELY AGREE				DO NOT AGREE AT ALL

IN THE TEAM I AM RATING:

11. I am fully committed to our team's goals.

| | 5 | 4 | 3 | 2 | 1 |

12. I am fully committed to making our team the best one possible.

| | 5 | 4 | 3 | 2 | 1 |

13. I am quite clear all the time about what really matters.

| | 5 | 4 | 3 | 2 | 1 |

14. My whole team is committed to the highest possible standards of quality in everything we deliver for someone else to use.

| | 5 | 4 | 3 | 2 | 1 |

15. Team members rarely let their personal feelings get in the way of getting the job done.

| | 5 | 4 | 3 | 2 | 1 |

16. Our team members rarely work by the clock; they do what's necessary to do the job right.

| | 5 | 4 | 3 | 2 | 1 |

17. We all keep the team's best interest uppermost in our minds.

| | 5 | 4 | 3 | 2 | 1 |

18. We all believe that what our team is doing is truly important.

| | 5 | 4 | 3 | 2 | 1 |

19. Our team members often make significant personal sacrifices to ensure the team's success.

| | 5 | 4 | 3 | 2 | 1 |

	COMPLETELY AGREE				DO NOT AGREE AT ALL

IN THE TEAM I AM RATING:

20. I am typically optimistic that we can get the job done – regardless of the obstacles.

| 5 | 4 | 3 | 2 | 1 |

21. It's easy to get help from other team members, when I need it.

| 5 | 4 | 3 | 2 | 1 |

22. Other team members go out of their way to help me succeed.

| 5 | 4 | 3 | 2 | 1 |

23. We are careful not to criticize any member to a third party.

| 5 | 4 | 3 | 2 | 1 |

24. We spend a lot more time praising the work of team members than we do finding fault with it.

| 5 | 4 | 3 | 2 | 1 |

25. When one team member has a personal problem and wants help, he/she can count on help from other team members.

| 5 | 4 | 3 | 2 | 1 |

26. We never surprise a team member in public with comments that might embarrass the member.

| 5 | 4 | 3 | 2 | 1 |

27. When any team member can't carry his/her share of the workload, other team members will always take up the slack.

| 5 | 4 | 3 | 2 | 1 |

	COMPLETELY AGREE				DO NOT AGREE AT ALL

IN THE TEAM I AM RATING:

28. We regularly help each other in our team to learn new competencies.

    5   4   3   2   1

29. If we get into conflicts in our team, we typically resolve them right away.

    5   4   3   2   1

30. We never take credit for someone else's work.

    5   4   3   2   1

31. We pride ourselves on doing a job better than most people typically expect.

    5   4   3   2   1

32. We never make excuses if anything our team does isn't right.

    5   4   3   2   1

33. Everything our team does represents me personally.

    5   4   3   2   1

34. We make sure that we get the feedback we need from our customers (internal and external) to ensure satisfying them.

    5   4   3   2   1

35. I feel a great deal of personal satisfaction from being a part of our team.

    5   4   3   2   1

36. Team members typically take any criticism of our team as a possible opportunity to improve.

    5   4   3   2   1

	COMPLETELY AGREE				**DO NOT AGREE AT ALL**

IN THE TEAM I AM RATING:

37.   We are our own most
severe critics.

	5	4	3	2	1

38.   We know exactly how
well we are doing at all
times.

	5	4	3	2	1

39.   I am very clear how
our team contributes
to the total success of
the organization.

	5	4	3	2	1

40.   We are typically
very positive to others
about our team's
performance.

	5	4	3	2	1

41.   Team members can
always be counted on
to do what they say
they will do.

	5	4	3	2	1

42.   We typically give
each other information
that is 100 per cent accurate.

	5	4	3	2	1

43.   When team members
don't know something,
they will always tell
you they don't and not
act as if they do.

	5	4	3	2	1

44.   When a team member
doesn't agree with
another team member, he/
she will let the other
member know – regardless
of the other member's
position or rank.

	5	4	3	2	1

	COMPLETELY AGREE				DO NOT AGREE AT ALL

IN THE TEAM I AM RATING:

45. Our team members always keep sensitive team business within the team.

	5	4	3	2	1

46. Our team members typically demonstrate the highest form of personal honesty and integrity.

	5	4	3	2	1

47. Team members rarely conceal anything from another member that they feel the member should know.

	5	4	3	2	1

48. It's safe to give the team bad news when I must.

	5	4	3	2	1

49. There are very good reasons if any member fails to fulfil a commitment.

	5	4	3	2	1

50. You can get a straight answer from anyone about anything you want to know.

	5	4	3	2	1

END

KINLAW ASSOCIATES
255 College Cross, No. 77
Norfolk, Virginia 23510

Author: Dennis C. Kinlaw, Ed.D.

SUPERIOR TEAM DEVELOPMENT INVENTORY: PART 4

FOCUSING ON LEADERSHIP

Directions

In completing the **Superior Team Development Inventory: Part 4** you must be consistent about the 'team' you are rating. The team you are rating consists of you and all the other people who are involved with you as a team in the **Superior Team Development System**.

Follow the steps below and complete this part of the **Inventory**.

1. Indicate the company or organization to which you belong, e.g., Aerospace Technical Services, Last National Bank, Speedy Supply, etc. and the date on which you are completing this part of the **Superior Team Development Inventory (STDI)**.

Company/Organization _____ Date _____

2. Name the team on which you are completing the STDI.

Team _____

3. Each item in the STDI presents a characteristic that may describe your team to some degree or which may not describe your team at all. Indicate the degree to which you believe the item accurately describes your own team by circling the appropriate number on the scale (5 to 1) that appears with each item. '5' indicates that you completely agree. '1' indicates that you do not agree at all.

4. Complete **every** item.

5. Follow any special instructions that your team may have established for turning in and scoring your completed STDI: Part 4.

CONTINUE TO NEXT PAGE

	COMPLETELY AGREE				DO NOT AGREE AT ALL

THE LEADER(S) IN THE TEAM I AM RATING:

1. Ensures that the team takes the time it needs to work on its own development.

5	4	3	2	1

2. Makes it clear to everyone that team development must be considered part of everyone's job.

5	4	3	2	1

3. Initiates training to help team members develop the skills they need to function as a superior team.

5	4	3	2	1

4. Is quick to acknowledge people who perform as team players.

5	4	3	2	1

5. Regularly affirms his/her commitment to team development.

5	4	3	2	1

6. Takes the lead in helping the team set targets to improve itself as a team.

5	4	3	2	1

7. Takes the lead in having the team evaluate its performance.

5	4	3	2	1

8. Encourages team members to use the competencies of each other.

5	4	3	2	1

	COMPLETELY AGREE				DO NOT AGREE AT ALL

**THE LEADER(S) IN THE TEAM
I AM RATING:**

9.   Encourages team
members to give him/her
feedback on his/her
performance as a team
member.

5	4	3	2	1

10.   Confronts others
positively when they
are not working as team
players.

5	4	3	2	1

11.   Viewed by other
members as an example of
what a team player should
be.

5	4	3	2	1

12.   Involves the rest of
the team in deciding about
new people being brought
into the team.

5	4	3	2	1

13.   Makes it easy for
others to disagree with
him/her.

5	4	3	2	1

14.   Involves the whole
team in making decisions
that affect the team.

5	4	3	2	1

15.   Always demonstrates
that he/she puts the team's
best interest above his/
her own.

5	4	3	2	1

16.   Always gives the team
the credit for achievements
rather than taking credit
himself/herself.

5	4	3	2	1

	COMPLETELY AGREE				DO NOT AGREE AT ALL

THE LEADER(S) IN THE TEAM I AM RATING:

17. Leads by gaining the commitment of team members to the team's goals.	5	4	3	2	1
18. Always encourages team members to resolve their own conflicts with each other before getting involved himself/herself.	5	4	3	2	1
19. Ensures that team members are recognized by upper management for their achievements.	5	4	3	2	1
20. Helps other members to participate fully at team meetings.	5	4	3	2	1
21. Makes it easy for others to be candid with him.	5	4	3	2	1
22. Gives his/her full attention to others when they are speaking.	5	4	3	2	1
23. Helps others to identify accurately problems for themselves.	5	4	3	2	1
24. Helps others take responsibility for solving their own problems.	5	4	3	2	1
25. Provides team members with practical career advice.	5	4	3	2	1

	COMPLETELY AGREE				DO NOT AGREE AT ALL

THE LEADER(S) IN THE TEAM I AM RATING:

26. Helps other members understand the expectations of senior managers.

5	4	3	2	1

27. Helps other team members identify the knowledge or skill they need to acquire.

5	4	3	2	1

28. Helps other team members gain expert status in their areas of responsibility.

5	4	3	2	1

29. Is very concrete in setting expectations with others about being team players.

5	4	3	2	1

30. Develops plans with others to improve their performances as team players.

5	4	3	2	1

END

Using the General Systems Model of Team Performance

The General Systems Model of Team Performance is found in Figure 4.3 in Chapter 4. In that chapter I listed and explained the elements in the model. Readers should refer to the model and the description of the elements as they follow the discussion below about using the model.

The General Systems Model of Team Performance helps teams to:

- identify a wide variety of improvement opportunities
- consider how improvements in one element of the system relate to changes in other elements of the system.

A wide variety of improvement opportunities

The model lends itself to the easy identification of improvement opportunities. Take, for example, how a team in the business of providing training might use the model. Suppose the team chose to concentrate on improving the information that it obtains from its customers by working on its customer communication link. What are some actions that the team might take?

The customer communication link, and all other such links, contains two actions: initiating (I) and receiving (R). The customer communication link consists of the many two-way communication connections that permit the team to: (1) measure how well its customers value what it delivers; (2) anticipate its customers' changing needs and requirements; and (3) discover with its customers how to improve every aspect of its services and products. Here are a few of the actions that a training team might take:

- conduct regular customer satisfaction surveys to determine quality of training, training needs, suggestions related to training design and delivery
- conduct post-training interviews with people attending training programmes

- conduct interviews with people who have a financial stake in the training
- conduct focus groups with people served by the training
- have customers compare the quality of the team's training programmes with other similar programmes
- track all customer complaints, keep tracking updated, and analyse and interpret on a very regular basis.

Suppose this training team wanted to concentrate on its own internal processes. It might analyse any of the following kinds of processes:

- the process for designing new training programmes
- the process for producing training materials
- the process of instructor preparation
- the process of participant accounting.

Or suppose the team focused on its outputs. Examples of outputs might be identified as profit from training programmes, trainee to trainer ratio, number of new customers or number of repeat customers. Suppose the team decided to work on profit from training programmes. Some strategies might be:

- compare overhead costs (trainer, travel, per diem, materials) to programme sale price
- compare overhead costs of one-day programmes and multiple-day programmes to programme sale prices
- analyse and compare competitor programmes to own programmes and weigh comparative strengths and weaknesses
- compare costs for alternative ways of producing training materials.

References and resources

Boreman, E. and Boreman, N. (1972), *Effective Small Group Communication*, Minneapolis: Burgess.

Boyett, J. and Conn, H. (1991), *Workplace 2000*, New York: Dutton.

Bradford, L. (1976), *Group Development*, San Diego: University Associates.

Bulker, P. (1986), 'Effects of team building and goal setting on productivity: a field experiment', *Academy of Management Journal*, **29**, (2): 305–28.

Cleland, D. (1996), *Strategic Management of Teams*, New York: John Wiley and Sons.

Ellis, C. and Tonkin, L. (1995) 'Survey report: mature teams rewards and the high-performance workplace: change and opportunity', *Target*, November/December: 6–14.

Gouillart, F. and Kelly, J. (1995), *Transforming the Organization*, New York: McGraw-Hill.

Hackman, J.R. (1983), 'A normative model of work team effectiveness', *Technical Report No. 2*, Research Program Group on Group Effectiveness, Yale School of Organization and Management, Arlington, VA: Office of Naval Research.

Hall, G., Rosenthal, J. and Wade, J. (1993), 'How to make re-engineering really work', *Harvard Business Review* November/December: 119.

Healy, D. (1989), *The Time of My Life*, Homewood, IL: Dow Jones Irwin.

Hensey, M. (1992), *Collective Excellence: Building Effective Teams* New York: American Society of Civil Engineers.

Johansen, R. (1996), *Upsizing the Individual in the Downsized Organization*, New York: Addison-Wesley.

Katzenbach, J. and Smith, D. (1993), *The Wisdom of Teams*, Boston Harvard Business School Press.

Kinlaw, D. (1989), *Coaching for Commitment*, San Diego, CA Pfeiffer and Company.

Kinlaw, D. (1990), *Trainer's Package: Coaching for Commitment*, San Diego, CA: Pfeiffer and Company.

Kinlaw, D. (1991), *Developing Superior Work Teams: Building Quality and the Competitive Edge*, New York: Lexington Books.

Kinlaw, D. (1991a), *Motivation Assessment Inventory*, Norfolk, VA Developmental Products.

Kinlaw, D. (1992), *Continuous Improvement and Measurement for Total Quality*, New York: Business One Irwin.

Kinlaw, D. (1993), *Team Managed Facilitation*, San Diego, CA Pfeiffer and Company.

Kinlaw, D. (1995), *The Practice of Empowerment*, Aldershot: Gower

Kinlaw, D. (1996), *ASTD Trainer's Sourcebook: Facilitation*, New York: Mc-Graw Hill.

Kinlaw, D. (1996a), *ASTD Trainer's Sourcebook: Coaching*, New York: Mc-Graw Hill.

Kinlaw, D. (1997), *Coaching: Winning Strategies for Individuals and Teams*, Aldershot: Gower.

Klein, J. (1984), 'Why supervisors resist employee involvement' *Harvard Business Review*, September/October: 87–95.

Kolodny, H. and Kiggundu, M. (1980), 'Towards the development of a sociotechnical systems model in woodlands mechanical harvesting', *Human Relations*, **33**: 623–45.

Lawler, E. (1986), *High Involvement Management*, San Francisco: Jossey-Bass.

Locke, E., Shaw, K., Saari, L. and Latham, G. (1981), 'Goal setting and task performance', *Psychological Bulletin 90*: 125–52.

Manz, C. and Sims, Jr. H. (1993), *Business Without Bosses*, New York: John Wiley and Sons.

Nieva, V., Fleishman, E. and Rieck, A. (1989), *Team Dimensions: Their Identity, Their Measurement and Their Relationships*, Alexandria, VA: U.S. Army Research Institute for the Behavioral and Social Sciences.

Osdenwald, S. (1996), *Global Solutions for Teams*, Chicago: Irwin.

Parker, G. (1991), 'Team players and teamwork', *Soundview Executive Book Summaries*, (4), April: 13.

Romig, D. (1996), *Breakthrough Teamwork*, Chicago: Irwin.

Rosen, N. (1989), *Teamwork and The Bottom Line*, Hilldale, NJ: Lawrence Erlbaum Associates.

Scherkenbach, W. (1988), *The Deming Route to Quality and Productivity*, Washington, DC: CeePress Books.

Schuster, H. (1990), *Teams for Quality Improvement*, Englewood Cliffs, NJ: Prentice Hall.

Semler, R. (1989), 'Creating work cultures with a competitive advantage', *Organizational Dynamics*, Winter: 5–27.

Shonk, J. (1992), *Team-Based Organizations*, Homewood, IL: Business One Irwin.

Steiner, I. (1972), *Group Process and Productivity*, New York: Academic Press.

Thamhain, H. and Wilemon D. (1987), 'Building high performing engineering project teams', *IEEE Transactions on Engineering Management*, EM-34 (3), August, 130–37.

Tjosvold, D. and Tjosvold, M. (1991), *Leading The Team Organization*, New York: Lexington Books.

Varney, G. (1989), *Building Productive Teams*, San Francisco: Jossey-Bass.

Wellins, R., Byham, W. and Dixon, G. (1994), *Inside Teams*, San Francisco: Jossey-Bass.

Werther, W. (1981), 'Productivity improvement through people', *Arizona Business*, February: 14–19.

Yankelovich, D. and Immerwahr, J. (1983), *Putting the Work Ethic to Work*, New York: The Public Agenda Foundation.

Zenger, J., Musselwhite, E., Hurson, K. and Perrin, C. (1994), *Leading Teams: Mastering the New Role*, Homewood, IL: Business One Irwin.

Index